Martin Lewis

Motive power

SN

FRENCH RAILWAYS

David Haydock

LONDON

IAN ALLAN LTD

First published 1986

ISBN 0 7110 1637 2

Published by Ian Allan Ltd, Shepperton, Surrey; and printed by Ian Allan Printing Ltd at its works at Coombelands in Runnymede, England

Front cover: 1,500V dc supply 5,375hp Class BB 7200 electric locomotive No BB 7312 is seen with the dual-current version of the design, 25kV ac/1,500V dc Class BB 22200 No BB 22305. *French Railways*

Back cover top: Side view of Class BB 66000 diesel-electric locomotive

Back cover centre: Side view of Class BB 16000 25kV ac electric locomotive

Back cover bottom: Side view of Class CC 21000 dual voltage 25kV ac/1,500V dc electric locomotive

All photographs are by the author unless otherwise stated

Glossary

CFL	Société Nationale des Chemins de Fer Luxembourgeois
DB	Deutsche Bundesbahn
LGV	Ligne à Grande Vitesse
RATP	Régie Autonome des Transports Parisiens
RER	Réseau Express Régional
SNCB	Société Nationale des Chemins de Fer Belges
SNCF	Société Nationale des Chemins de Fer Francais
TGV	Train à Grande Vitesse

Rolling Stock Builders

ANF	Ateliers du Nord de la France
CAFL	Compagnie des Ateliers et Forges de la Loire
CEM	Compagnie Electro-Mécanique
CFD	Chemins de Fer Départementaux
CIMT	Compagnie Industrielle de Matériel de Transport
MTE	Compagnie Matériel et Traction Electrique
SACM	Société Alsacienne de Construction Mécanique
SEMT	Chantiers de l'Atlantique
SG	Société Surgérienne de Constructions Mécaniques
SLM	Société Suisse pour la Construction de Locomotives et de Machines
SW	Société de Matériel Electrique SW

Introduction

Motive Power Recognition: SNCF covers the whole of the Société Nationale des Chemins de Fer Français (French National Railways) fleet of approximately 2,400 electric and 2,000 diesel locomotives, 800 diesel and gas turbine multiple units, 700 electric units, 100 TGV rakes and even its one operational steam loco. It does not contain details of the Paris RER and Metro, or other French metro systems, private railway motive power or that of the private companies which maintain SNCF's permanent way. Like other books in the series, it contains technical data on each class, details of differences within and between classes, advice on identification and, of course, a photograph of each variation where possible. It also gives as much detail as possible of workings and other information which provides a good background to the dry facts, in order that the reader may understand the French rail scene better. Of course, it has been impossible to include every detail difference but all the most important are covered.

Hopefully this book will give pleasure to any railway enthusiast visiting France and will stir an interest in a rail system which many claim to be the most modern and efficient in the world. The guide may even surprise some people who, perhaps, did not realise that as well as its well-publicised TGVs, SNCF has over 100 electric locomotives built before World War 2 and some stock dating back to 1908 still in regular passenger service.

I would like to thank SNCF staff for their assistance in preparing the book and I dedicate it to Fabienne and our new addition to the family.

David Haydock
Lille

The SNCF Network

This covers just over 21,500 route miles of which about 7,100 miles are electrified. This represents around one third of the network but these lines account for over 80% of total traffic. Before the creation of SNCF in 1937 2,270 miles of line were electrified, principally in the Paris suburbs at 750V dc third rail; also main lines south of Bordeaux/Toulouse and from Paris to Le Mans, Orléans and Limoges at 1,500V dc overhead. The first main SNCF schemes were to link up lines in the Southwest and to electrify the Paris-Dijon-Lyon main line. In the 1950s & 1960s came the large scale electrification of the Nord and Est region main lines which was done at 25kV ac. The oil crisis of 1973 produced the impetus for a few fill-in schemes such as Bordeaux-Toulouse, Narbonne-Cerbère and the Rhône left bank freight line at the original voltage. Where possible, now, electrification is at 25kV ac and bi-current locos are employed if necessary. This is the case with the Le Mans-Rennes/Nantes and Côte D'Azur schemes. With a squeeze on finance, and reducing returns, the pace of new electrification is now slowing down although, in order for the full benefit of the TGV-Atlantique to be reaped, the lines St Brieuc-Brest, Rennes-Quimper, Nantes-Redon and Poitiers-La Rochelle will be 'sparked' in the late 1980s or early 1990s. The only other major electrification project at present is the Paris-Nevers-Clermont Ferrand main line, which is scheduled for completion by 1992.

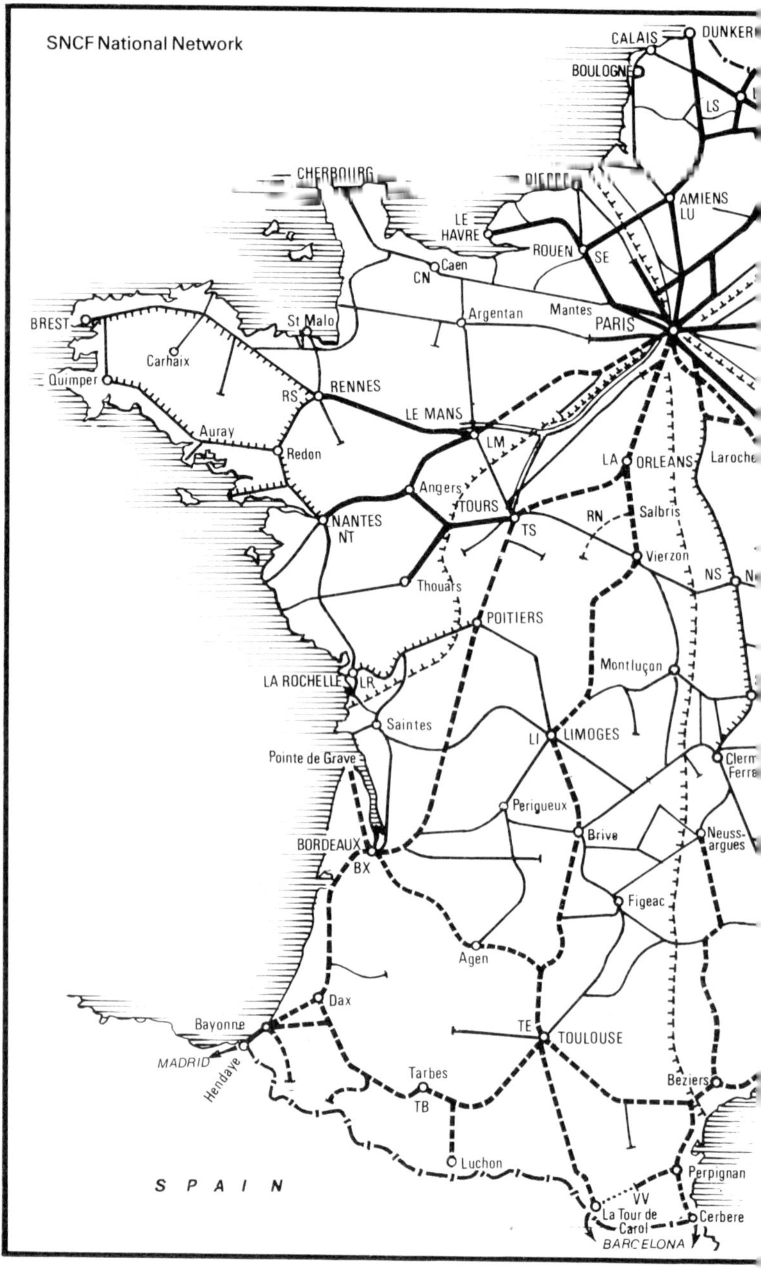
SNCF National Network
CALAIS
DUNKERQUE
BOULOGNE
LS
CHERBOURG
LE HAVRE
ROUEN
SE
AMIENS
LU
Caen
CN
Argentan
Mantes
PARIS
BREST
St Malo
Carhaix
Quimper
RS
RENNES
LE MANS
LM
Auray
Redon
LA
ORLEANS
Laroche
Angers
TOURS
NANTES
NT
TS
RN
Salbris
Vierzon
NS
Thouars
POITIERS
Montluçon
LA ROCHELLE
LR
Saintes
LI
LIMOGES
Pointe de Grave
Perigueux
Brive
Neuss-argues
BORDEAUX
BX
Figeac
Agen
Dax
Bayonne
MADRID
Hendaye
TE
TOULOUSE
Tarbes
TB
Beziers
Luchon
Perpignan
SPAIN
VV
La Tour de Carol
Cerbere
BARCELONA

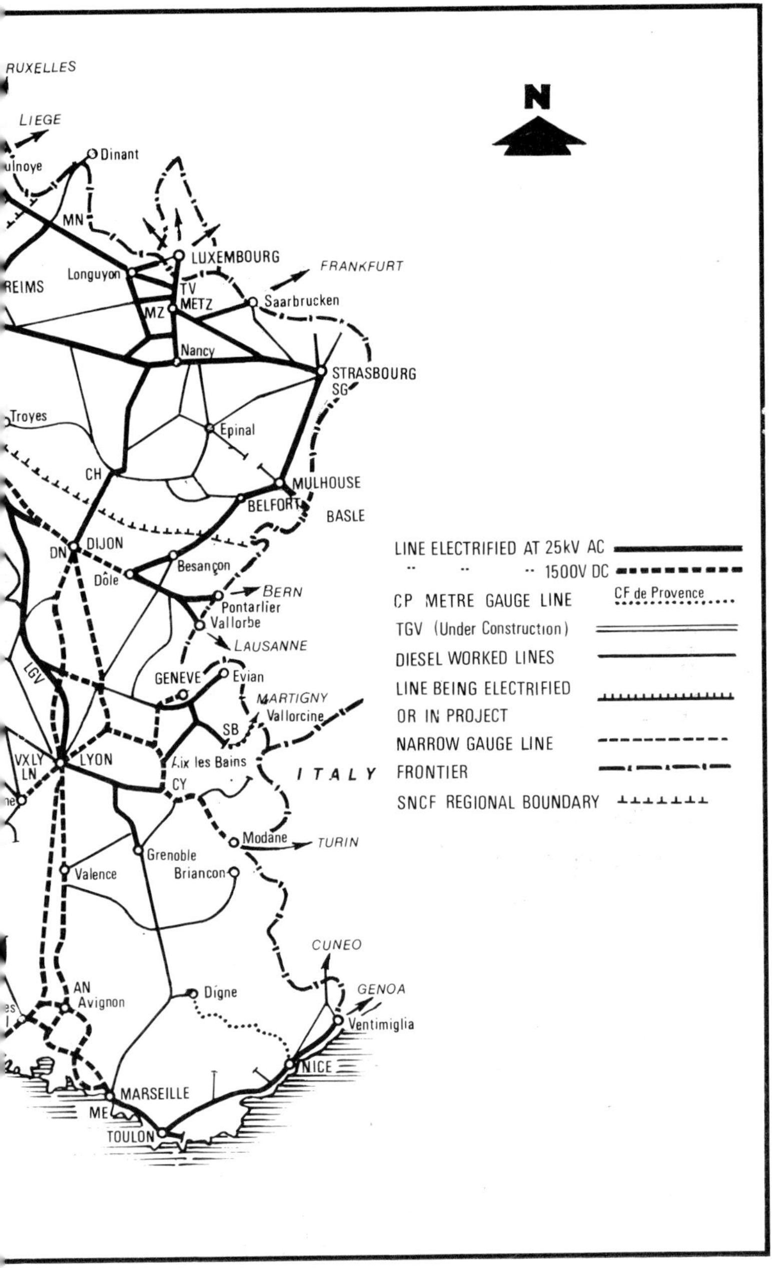
RUXELLES
LIEGE
Dinant
ulnoye
MN
LUXEMBOURG
FRANKFURT
Longuyon
TV
METZ
MZ
REIMS
Saarbrucken
Nancy
STRASBOURG
SG
Troyes
Epinal
CH
MULHOUSE
BELFORT
BASLE
DIJON
DN
Besançon
Dôle
BERN
Pontarlier
Vallorbe
LAUSANNE
LGV
GENEVE
Evian
MARTIGNY
Vallorcine
SB
LYON
VXLY
LN
Aix les Bains
ITALY
CY
Modane
TURIN
Grenoble
Valence
Briancon
CUNEO
GENOA
AN
Avignon
Digne
Ventimiglia
NICE
MARSEILLE
ME
TOULON
N
LINE ELECTRIFIED AT 25kV AC
" " " 1500V DC
CP METRE GAUGE LINE
CF de Provence
TGV (Under Construction)
DIESEL WORKED LINES
LINE BEING ELECTRIFIED OR IN PROJECT
NARROW GAUGE LINE
FRONTIER
SNCF REGIONAL BOUNDARY

The Paris Region

As well as an extensive SNCF network in Paris, there are also the RATP (Paris Transport Authority) concerns, the Metro and RER (Regional Express Network). Although the Metro is not the concern of this book, the RER is important as SNCF operates some of the services either on its own or jointly with RATP, and because future RER lines will be formed by linking some SNCF lines to the present system. Passenger traffic in Paris is very heavy as the figures show. SNCF termini are of varied importance in handling this traffic, but Saint Lazare is by far the busiest, handling about 400,000 passengers a day including about 50,000 in the hour between 08.00 and 09.00 and again between 17.30 and 18.30. This puts it among the busiest five in the world.

The whole passenger network in Paris is electrified except for the St Ouen-Ermont-Eaubonne line which is in the process of being wired. The network has not finished expanding either. At present, a new loop line is being built to serve the new town of Cergy and this will be linked to line A of the RER at Nanterre in 1987. Also to the west of Paris, a new branch of RER line C will be created in 1987 via the St Ouen line to Montigny Beauchamp. Towards the end of the decade, the creation of an additional tunnel from Chatelet to Gare de Lyon low-level, will allow services from Orry la Ville on the line from Gare du Nord to be interconnected with those from Gare de Lyon to Melun to form line D of the RER. Projects on the drawing board at present are the re-electrification of the last standard gauge third-rail line in France, Issy Plaine-Puteaux, with extension to La Défense, and the reopening of part of the 'Grande Ceinture' (the almost circular freight route which passes round the outskirts of Paris) between Sartrouville and Val de Fontenay to passenger traffic. As the latter scheme will involve the tripling or quadrupling of this busy freight route it is likely to take some time to complete. To complete the list of new construction in progress or proposed, it is necessary to mention the station at Saint Michel on RER line B. This is a very important improvement as it will allow interchange between lines B and C, thus taking some pressure off the Metro.

Finally, for the incurable gricers amongst readers, it should be pointed out that although many locations in Paris are busy vantage points, Juvisy and Villeneuve Saint Georges are exceptionally animated. Indeed, at these locations it is possible to see virtually every dc electric class and a large number of other locomotives. Just one word of caution, though. It is officially forbidden to take photographs in SNCF stations and a permit should be obtained from SNCF headquarters.

TGV No 08 at Paris Gare de Lyon. C.Davis

Lines in the Paris Region

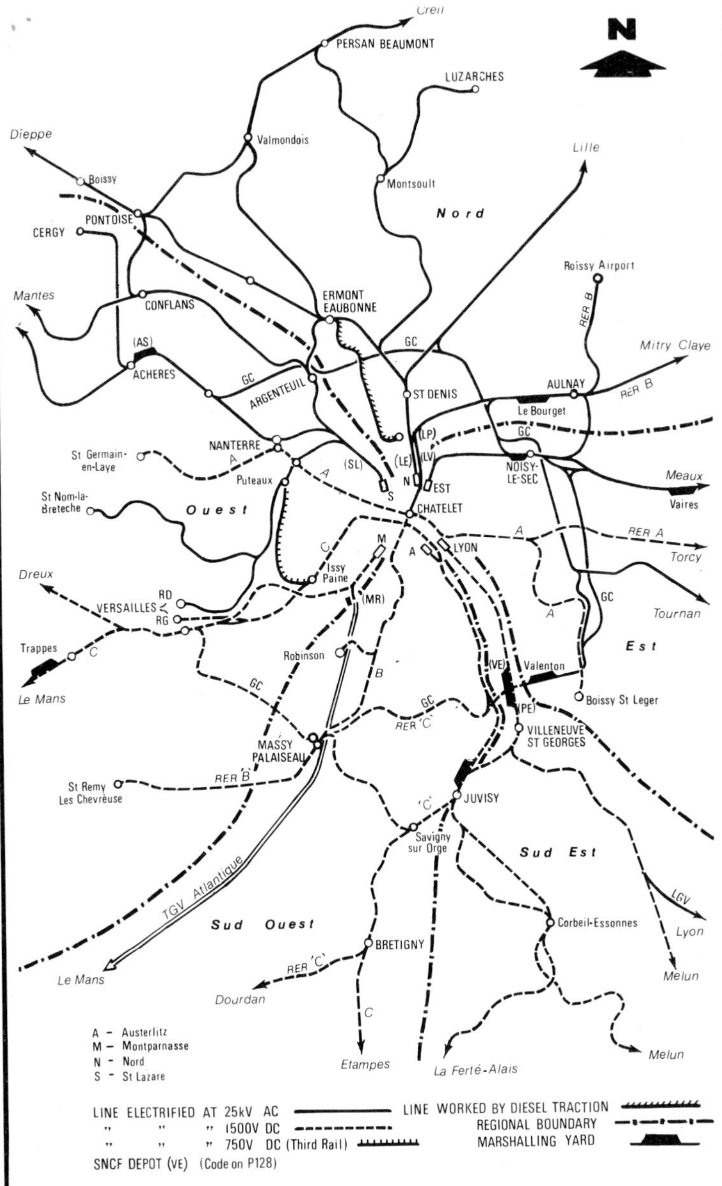

The Railway Scene in the Channel Ports

For most visitors, their first glimpse of France will be at one of the channel ports of north-west France. Indeed, many people are now making day trips to Calais, Boulogne or Dunkerque, usually with shopping in mind. Railway enthusiasts buying their booze and baguettes might consider a period of SNCF-watching in the time they have left before the ferry leaves. Alternatively, those making longer journeys might be interested in what they can see around these three towns.

Dunkerque

Dunkerque is the furthest east and the largest of the three, being the third largest port in France after Marseille and Le Havre. Rail handles around 20 million tonnes of freight there each year, although passenger traffic is not very significant. Passengers for the continent arrive at Dunkerque Ouest which is, in fact, almost 10 miles from the town and squeezed somewhere between the nuclear power station and oil refinery. Sealink operate a train ferry from here to Dover which has been in danger of being withdrawn recently. The yard serving the train ferry is shunted by two A1AA1A 62000s, which are SNCFs oldest diesel class and rapidly disappearing. Ouest station has recently lost its only passenger service, the 'Night Ferry' to the Newhaven-Dieppe route.

Between Ouest and Ville is situated Dunkerque's main marshalling yard, Grande Synthe, which is conveniently placed close to the area's hypermarket. Traffic to and from the yard is handled by A1AA1A 62000, BB 63000, BB 66000 and BB 66400 on local freights and shunting, BB 12000, CC 14100, BB 16000 and BB 16500 on long distance work, and perhaps the occasional BB 13000, BB 17000, BB 25500 or BB 67400. From Dunkerque Ville, express passenger trains are hauled by Class BB 16000 while local push-pull trains towards Arras and Lille are powered by BB 16500s. Trains to Calais, of which there are only four a day (!), and a few other local stopping trains are covered by Class X 4500 DMUs. Of particular interest are the CC 14100s and A1AA1A 62000s which are both being withdrawn. This area is one of the last strongholds of the A1AA1A 62000 class, roughly 10 of which work around Grande Synthe.

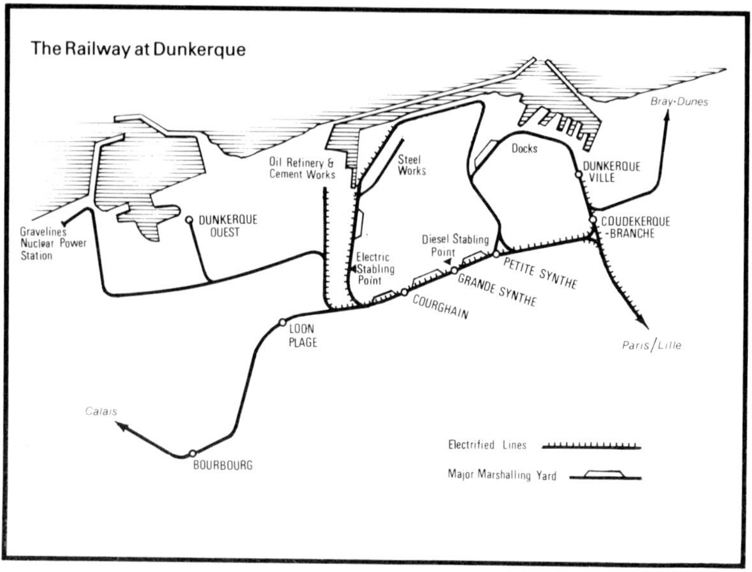

Calais

In contrast to Dunkerque, the port of Calais is very important for its passenger traffic (approaching 8 million a year by all modes) but handles a relatively insignificant traffic in freight. As the area is not electrified, only diesel classes can be seen here. Longueau-based BB 67400s, usually in pairs, take forward all express passenger trains and some freight while local passenger trains are formed of either Class X 4500 DMUs or push-pull stock and BB 66400s. This class also works freight together with BB 63500 and BB 66000 locomotives based at Longueau. Most trains begin or terminate at Calais Ville station, but twice a day in each direction there are boat trains which continue to or from Maritime. Because of the relative lack of variety in motive power and traffic at Calais, it is the least interesting of the three channel ports.

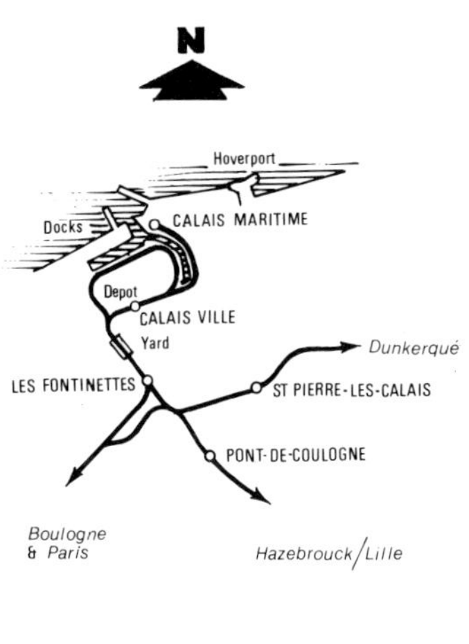

The Railway at Calais

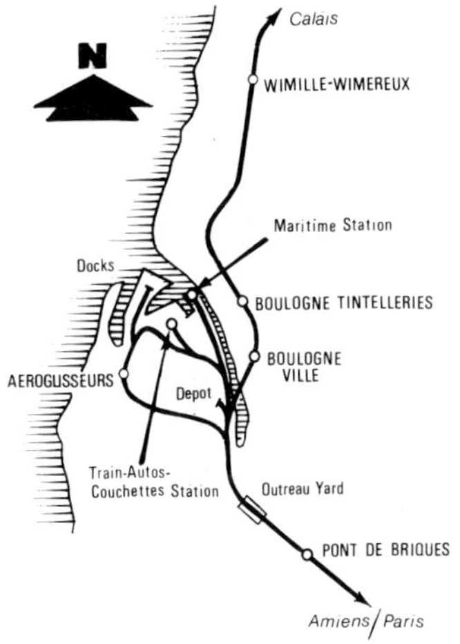

The Railway at Boulogne

Boulogne

Boulogne is the first major stop for trains from Calais to Paris and thus sees many of the same trains as Calais. However, Boulogne also generates its own passenger traffic, particularly at the hoverport, which is served by Aeroglisseurs station. Between there and Paris there are up to five trains a day which are formed of Class T 2000 gas turbine units based at Caen in Normandy. Maritime station is only used sporadically, but is of interest as it is served by the 'Orient Express'. At present, this train operates twice a week in summer and once a week in winter and is an impressive sight with two BB 67400s at its head. Boulogne TAC station is served by sections of long-distance trains serving the south of France and Italy. The main station for the town is Boulogne Ville, and here can be seen Classes BB 63500, BB 66000, BB 66400, BB 67400 as well as a variety of shunters and Class X 4500 DMUs. Freight is not very important in this area and is mainly connected to the functioning of the steelworks close to the hoverport.

SNCF Traffic

The SNCF network carried 736 million passengers in 1983, this being equivalent to over 36,000 million passenger miles, of which 78% is represented by passengers on express trains. The Paris suburban network accounted for 456 million passengers but only 5,000 million passenger miles. Passenger traffic has been increasing gently but steadily in recent years, although most of the growth has been generated by TGV services and some slight reductions have been evident on certain other routes. Express average speeds are high and are continually being raised. At present, 5,300 miles of the network are passable at 160km/h (99mph) or more. About 1,000 miles are passed for 200km/h running, routes concerned being Paris-Nantes, Bordeaux and Toulouse, and Lyon-Avignon, although the latter only for TGV units.

176 million tonnes of freight was hauled by SNCF in 1983. That gives 36,900 million tonne miles, giving an average haul length of over 200 miles – much longer than in Britain where the majority of freight is short-distance power station coal. In fact, SNCF carries half of all freight travelling over 30 miles in France. Freight is carried to three main formulae: RA (Régime Accélerée) – fast transits at up to 120km/h (75mph) for perishables and finished products with a high value; RO (Régime Ordinaire) – cheaper but slower than RA; block trains (trains complets) for offered traffic of 1,500-3,000 tonnes. This traffic accounts for 48% of total tonnage. Two features make French rail freight somewhat different from that in Britain. Firstly, there is much less coal transported as France has few large remaining deposits and has a large nuclear power programme. However, SNCF carries far more food/agricultural products than BR, eg wine, mineral water and cereals, a traffic which has grown by almost a half in the last 10 years.

Motive Power Trends

In the next five years developments will be largely influenced by work on the TGV-Atlantique project. In the short term this will mean the revitalisation of diesel Classes CC 65000 and CC 65500 which will be needed for works trains. In the longer term it will mean large scale redeployment of electric and diesel locomotives and units.

Apart from the TGV-A, the greatest innovation will be the introduction of 'universal' bi-current Class BB 26000 which should start late in 1986, allowing the withdrawal of certain very old electric classes through 'cascading'. The continuing delivery of double-deck EMUs of Class Z 8800 to the Paris region will allow older EMUs to be transferred or withdrawn and replace hauled stock thus freeing Class BB 8500 locos. The delivery of 'Z2' EMUs of Classes Z 9600 and Z 11500 will displace DMUs working 'under the wires' and through reallocation permit the elimination of Classes X 2400, X 2700 & X 3800. The introduction of new single units of Class X 2200 will also help this along. Finally, declining traffic in heavy industrial freight will put at risk several older classes, particularly BB 13000 & CC 14100.

One more possible influence on the evolution of the fleet will be the increase of the maximum speed for 'Régime Accélérée' freight trains from 90 to 100km/h. Not only will this involve modifications to classes with a 'PV' speed of 90km/h but it may also mean a slight reduction in the fleet if higher speeds bring better locomotive utilisation.

Foreign Locomotive Workings

As France has frontiers with six other countries, it is not surprising that some interworking is practised between national networks. In some cases, this is only a matter of a couple of miles across the border, but in others, longer distances are involved. Details of SNCF locos working into neighbouring countries are given for individual classes. Foreign locomotives which cross deep into France include SNCB (Belgian Railways) Class 51 diesels which work from Brussels to Lille, SNCB Class 15, 16 & 18 electric locomotives from Brussels to Paris Nord and DB (German Railways) Class 181 electrics which get as far as Metz and Strasbourg.

Depots

A list of SNCF depots is given on page 128.

Notes on Class Details

SNCF Numbering System

All SNCF numbers are prefixed by one or more letters. In the case of main line locomotives, this always denotes the wheel arrangement (BB 300 is a Bo-Bo, and so on). All shunter numbers (except the four shunters used on the metre-gauge Salbris-Buzançais line which are officially classified with a T-prefix, for no apparent reason, but actually carry BA) are prefixed by the letter Y. Diesel multiple unit numbers are prefixed by an X, EMU numbers by Z, gas turbine units by T and TGVs by the letters TGV. In the case of all multiple units, this first letter is followed by an R (standing for remorque) on trailer cars. Multiple unit coaches also carry other letters before the number denoting the arrangement of the vehicle:

A first class seating
B second class seating
D baggage compartment
P postal compartment
r Restauration
u Air Conditioning
x Driving Trailer

So, for example, XBD 4301 is a DMU power car with second class seating and a baggage compartment. ZRABx 16006 is an EMU driving trailer with first and second class seats.

Numbering follows the following rules: 1,500V dc electrics are numbered 1-9999, 25kV ac electrics 10000-19999, bi-current electrics 20000-29999, tri-current electrics (none exists at present) 30000-39999 and quadri-current electrics are 40000-49999. The 0-99 numbers of each group are reserved for prototypes. Light diesel shunters (locotracteurs) are 1-9999 again, heavy diesel shunters (the last have just been scrapped) are 50000-59999 and main line diesels 60000-89999. Non-electric units are numbered as follows: 1-999 metre gauge DMUS, 1000-2099 gas turbine units, 2100-9999 conventional DMUs. EMUs are 1-999 for metre gauge units and 1000-9999 for standard gauge. TGVs are, at present, numbered 23000 up for dual-current units and 33000 for tri-current units. Finally, units which have been purchased by 'third-parties' have a 9 prefix to previously indicated number series. The figure in brackets after each series of loco or unit numbers represents the number in service. This system has now been revised as it creates duplication *but* no existing numbers will be changed.

Former Numbers

It can be seen from the original numbers of older diesel types that SNCF used to have a numbering system which is strange to the British eye. This was a continuation of the system used for classification of steam locomotives which was done by *axles* rather than wheels. Under this system, a British 4-6-2 would be classified as a 231. So, SNCF's first diesels were classified as 040 for Bo-Bos and 060 for Co-Cos, followed by a two letter code DA, DB, DC and so on, followed by a serial number. This system was replaced by the present one in the early 1960s.

Former Owners of SNCF Locomotives

SNCF came into being in 1937, railways in France previously being owned by a small number of large companies. Locomotives still remain from three of these:

PO Chemin de Fer de Paris-Orléans (which covered the Paris-Orléans and Paris-Limoges main lines)
Midi Compagnie du Midi (which covered the far south west of France)
Etat Chemin de Fer de l'Etat (which covered an area similar to the Ouest region of SNCF)

Wheel Arrangements

SNCF and the French railway industry have long been leaders in the development of 'monomotor' bogies where the drive to two or even three axles comes from one centrally placed motor. These locos are of type B-B or C-C, whereas those locos which have independently powered axles are Bo-Bo, Co-Co, etc. In the case of monomotor bogied locos, two maximum speeds are usually given. This is because the bogies' gear ratio can be changed while the loco is at rest in order to adapt the engine for freight or passenger work. The lower speed, for freight or passenger trains on difficult lines, is called PV (petite vitesse) and the higher speed GV (grande vitesse).

SNCF Classes

*Metre Gauge

Class BB 300

Number series: BB 301-BB 355 (49)
Former numbers: PO Railway 241-264, SNCF 0325-0355
Built by: Siemens (301-307), Alsthom (308-344), Schneider Jeumont (345-355)
Introduced: 1938-39 (301-324) 1946-48 (325-355)
Type: Bo-Bo
Length: 12.93m (42ft 5in)
Wheelbase: 8.95m (29ft 4in)
Wheel diameter: 1.35m (4ft 5in)
Weight in running order: 76-80 tonnes
UIC power rating: 1,240kW (1,665hp)
Maximum speed:
75km/h (47mph) manoeuvres
105km/h (65mph) main line
Pantograph type: PO Type M diamond
Nominal supply voltage: 1,500V dc
Depots of allocation: PS, CY, VE, LN, MR, TS
Works responsible: Béziers
Livery: Dark green with red buffer beams. 325-355 lined in white with red SNCF roundel

This is one of five very old classes of low-powered electric locomotives built at the time of the electrification of the 1,500V dc network in the southwestern part of France, which are still in service. Like Classes BB 4200 & BB 4700, most have now been converted from main line locomotives to be used for what the French call 'manoeuvres' – shunting and ECS work.

The class was built in two batches with the War in between. The main difference between batches is the front end design, BB 301-BB 324 having a door in the front and three cab windows. All this first batch are now converted for 'manoeuvres' and are mostly allocated to PS and VE depots for work around Paris Lyon and Austerlitz stations. In the photograph BB 301 is seen on Paris Sud Ouest depot.

The second batch differs from the first in having two large windows and no door in the front end as well as in having a prominent box on the left-hand cab side. This batch have not all been converted for 'manoeuvres' work and some will remain at TS depot until 1988, working main line freight, like No BB 330, seen at Salbris in early 1985. These locos will soon be withdrawn leaving most of the batch working shunting duties, mainly in the Lyon area. The conversion to 'manoeuvres' includes the reduction of their gear ratio and the installation of radio telephones. On the photograph of BB 331 in the Lyon Mouche roundhouse the aerial can be seen clearly, as can the box on the left-hand side of the cab.

Class BB 900

Number series: BB 901-BB 935 (7)
Former numbers: Etat Railway 101-135
Built by: Alsthom
Introduced: 1936-37
Type: Bo-Bo
Length: 12.87m (42ft 3in)
Wheelbase: 8.95m (29ft 4in)
Wheel diameter: 1.4m (4ft 7in)
Weight in running order: 79 tonnes
UIC power rating: 1,200kW (1,610hp)
Maximum speed: 105km/h (65mph)
Pantograph type: Faiveley G diamond
Nominal supply voltage: 1,500V dc
Depot of allocation: LI
Works responsible: No longer overhauled
Livery: Dark green lined in yellow with red buffer beams

Like BB 300, this class dates from the original electrification of lines in southern France. Unlike BB 300, they are not being retained for shunting work and will be withdrawn by the end of 1986. Until then, they may be seen on freight workings on the Paris-Toulouse main line, although their level of activity is not likely to be very high. The best places to see them will be between Limoges and Cahors although they occasionally descend to Toulouse. In many ways, these locos are similar to Class BB 300, particularly when viewed from the side. Originally, their front end design was very close to the first batch of BB 300, but later the class was rebuilt without a door in the front end but with three windows. This plus the lack of jumper cables on the nose differentiates them from the other similar classes still in service. Here is BB 908 on Villeneuve depot. It will soon be time for this loco to STOP!

Class CC 1100

Number series: CC 1101-CC 1112 (12)
Former numbers: PO Railway 1001-1012
Built by: Compagnie Générale de Construction de Locomotives/Oerlikon
Introduced: 1937-48
Type: C-C
Length: 17.19m (56ft 5in)
Wheelbase: 12.3m (40ft 4in)
Wheel diameter: 1.4m (4ft 7in)
Weight in running order: 91 tonnes
UIC power rating: 400kW (540hp)
Maximum speed: 25km/h (16mph)
Pantograph type: PO Type M diamond
Nominal supply voltage: 1,500V dc
Depots of allocation: VE, TS, LN, TE
Works responsible: Béziers
Livery: Dark green with red buffer beams and window frames

This is the only class of electric locomotives on SNCF's books which was built specifically for shunting duties. This explains the convenient central cab, the coupling rods, very low gearing and the moderately heavy weight. These locos are rarely seen away from their traditional duties of hump shunting long rakes of wagons in the marshalling yards at Villeneuve, St Pierre des Corps, Lyon (Sibelin) and Toulouse St Jory. Here, CC 1104 is seen at work in Villeneuve yard.

Class BB 4100

Number series: BB 4104-BB 4193 (8)
Former numbers: Midi Railway Class 4100 and 4600 locomotives
Built by: Constructions Electrique de France
Introduced: 1928-32
Type: Bo-Bo
Length: 12.87m (42ft 3in)
Wheelbase: 8.95m (29ft 4in)
Wheel diameter: 1.4m (4ft 7in)
Weight in running order: 78 tonnes
UIC power rating: 1,160kW (1,560hp)
Maximum speed: 75km/h (47mph)
Pantograph type: Faiveley type D diamond
Nominal supply voltage: 1,500V dc
Depots of allocation: TE, AN
Works responsible: No longer overhauled
Livery: Dark green

This class has remained active on freight during the past few years on two particular lines: Toulouse-La Tour de Carol and Béziers-Neussargues. By 1986, only two units, Nos BB 4119 and BB 4123 will remain on the former line as they have been specially fitted with snowploughs for work on the upper part of the line above Foix. On the latter line, all workings will disappear during the year and the AN locos which ply the line will be withdrawn. However BB 4175 will be retained for the French railway museum in Mulhouse. This photo shows BB 4116, a 55 year old veteran, taking a rest on Toulouse depot.

Class BB 4200

Number series: BB 4206-BB 4249 (16)
Former numbers: Midi Railway Class 4200 renumbered out of order
Built by: Alsthom
Introduced: 1933-35
Type: Bo-Bo
Length: 12.87m (42ft 3in)
Wheelbase: [illegible]
Wheel diameter: 1.4m (4ft 7in)
Weight in running order: 75 tonnes
UIC power rating: 1,160kW (1,560hp)
Maximum speed: 75km/h (47mph)
Pantograph type: Faiveley type D diamond
Nominal supply voltage: 1,500V dc
Depots of allocation: PS TF TS
Works responsible: Beziers
Livery: Dark green with red buffer beams

This class was converted from the same group of Midi Railway locos as Class BB 4700 and is identical to them except for having a lower gear ratio and, thus, a lower maximum speed. Originally main line engines, the whole class was, like the BB 300s, recently downgraded to 'manoeuvres' and can now be seen at work in stations and marshalling yards on the line out of Paris Austerlitz and around Toulouse. Here, No BB 4231 is seen on station pilot duties, shunting DMU trailer vehicles at Toulouse Matabiau.

Class BB 4700

Number series: BB 4730-BB 4777 (45)
Former numbers: Midi Railway Class 4200 renumbered
Built by: Alsthom
Introduced: 1933-35
Type: Bo-Bo
Length: 12.87m (42ft 3in)
Wheelbase: 8.95m (29ft 4in)
Wheel diameter: 1.4m (4ft 7in)
Weight in running order: 75 tonnes
UIC power rating: 1,160kW (1,560hp)
Maximum speed: 90km/h (56mph)
Pantograph type: Faiveley Type D diamond
Nominal supply voltage: 1,500V dc
Depots of allocation: BX, TS, TB, LI, PS, LA
Works responsible: Béziers
Livery: Dark green with red buffer beams

Because of their common origins, the BB 4700 class looks identical to Class BB 4200, the differences being hidden from view. This class has the same sort of duties as BB 4200 but is wider spread throughout the Sud Ouest region. They can be seen in all large stations and marshalling yards in the division with the exception of Toulouse. BB 4774 is seen here between duties on Paris Sud Ouest depot.

Class CC 6500

Number series: CC 6501-CC 6574 (74)
Built by: Alsthom/MTE
Introduced: 1969-75
Type: C-C
Length: 20.19m (66ft 3in)
Wheelbase: 15.206m (49ft 11in)
Wheel diameter: 1.14m (3ft 9in)
Weight in running order: 115-120 tonnes
UIC power rating: 5,900kW (7,930hp)
Maximum speed: PV 100km/h (62mph) GV 200km/h (124mph)
Pantograph type: AM18B single arm
Nominal supply voltage: 1,500V dc
Depots of allocation: PS, LN
Works responsible: Oullins
Livery: Silver grey with red panel on sides and noses lined in orange. Dark grey round cab windows. 6539-6559 see below.

This class was built in three batches which can be distinguished from each other by the design of lateral grilles. The original batch, CC 6501-CC 6538, have horizontal grilles designed to harmonize well with the very long angular body painted in 'Trans Europ Express' livery. As can be seen from the photo of CC 6518 *Orléans* at Toulouse depot (below) this still looks very modern today, over 15 years after the class was introduced. Most of this batch are allocated to PS depot and work all the fastest passenger trains on the Sud Ouest region including Corail 200 trains at 200km/h. For this they are, unlike Lyon-based members, fitted with 'préannonce' cab signalling. The detection equipment is fitted just to the rear of one bogie and can be seen clearly opposite on No CC 6524. PS members also work other, less glamorous, passenger trains as well as a small number of express freights. These workings take them over all the division's electrified main lines as well as along the south coast to Marseille.

The second batch, Nos CC 6539-CC 6559, has a long, deep, square lateral grille, which is less in keeping with the general looks of the locomotive. These engines were originally built for work on the steep and tortuous 'Maurienne' line from Chambéry to Modane, which is an international artery continuing to Turin. At the time of their construction, the line was electrified by third rail and so they were fitted with both collector shoes and pantographs for through working on the rest of the Sud Est network. These 21 locomotives were also restricted to 100km/h and, as can be seen from this photo of CC 6557 at Villeneuve St Georges, have a more austere livery of blue/green lined out in white. All but the first five of this batch are fitted with mini snowploughs. The Maurienne line has now been re-electrified at 1,500V dc overhead and so the batch have lost their collector shoes and can now work at 100 or 200km/h like the rest. The whole batch is allocated to Lyon Mouche and shares a diagram with most of the final batch.

The batch which used to work the Maurienne line are now appearing in the standard silver-grey and red livery of the class after major overhauls, although the majority still remain in blue/green. The illustration shows No CC 6555, one of the first to be repainted, on show at an open day at Lille – a long way from its normal stamping ground!

The final batch, CC 6560-CC 6574, have slightly shallower rectangular lateral grilles. Originally built to haul the most important passenger trains on the Sud Est region, they have now lost most of this work, either because of the introduction of TGVs or to Class BB 7200, which are less expensive to operate. However, their high power rating is particularly appreciated for overnight international passenger trains which often have over 16 vehicles. Apart from these their passenger stronghold is the Chambéry-Modane line on trains between Lyon and Turin. They are also common on the same route hauling freight, and are seen more frequently on Chambéry depot than at Lyon, which is their home. No CC 6572 *Résistance Fer* is illustrated returning from a Lyon-Turin working on a three coach stopping train from Modane to Chambéry.

Classes CC 7000 and CC 7100

Number series: CC 7001/2 (2)
CC 7101-CC 7158 (46)
Built by: Alsthom/CEM/Fives Lille
Introduced: 7001/2 1949
7101-7158 1952-55
Type: Co-Co
Length: 7001/2 18.83m (61ft 9in)
7101-58 18.922m (62ft 1in)
Wheelbase: 14.14m (46ft 5in)
Wheel diameter: 1.25m (4ft 1in)
Weight in running order: 105-107 tonnes
UIC power rating:
7001/2 2,770kW (3,720hp)
7101-43 3,490kW (4,690hp)
7144-58 3,240kW (4,350hp)
Maximum speed: 140km/h (87mph)
Pantograph type: Faiveley G diamond
Nominal supply voltage: 1,500V dc
Depot of allocation: AN
Works responsible: No longer overhauled
Livery: Pale blue above and darker blue below waistline with bright blue between the double aluminium flashes

This was the first class of express electric locomotive in France with all axles powered, appearing after a series of 2D2 designs culminating in the 2D2 9100s. Originally used on crack passenger expresses, they have been displaced onto freight duties although retaining a few local passenger workings and being active on relief passenger trains at peak times such as the ski season. All locomotives, including the two prototypes, CC 7001/2, are outwardly identical and the class shares a common diagram from AN depot despite differences in power rating, gear ratio and final drive between batches. The class is due to be withdrawn over the next 10 years but, for the moment, can be seen almost anywhere on the Sud Est dc network as well as at Cerbère and Toulouse on the Sud Ouest. No CC 7107, which jointly holds the world speed record for an electric locomotive of 331km/h (206mph), has been withdrawn and will be displayed at special exhibitions before going to the Mulhouse railway museum. Here, No CC 7113 is seen running light through Villeneuve Saint Georges.

Class BB 7200

Number series: BB 7201-BB 7440 (239)
Built by: Alsthom/MTE
Introduced: 1976-85
Type: B-B
Length: 17.48m (57ft 4in)
Wheelbase: 12.494m (41ft 0in)
Wheel diameter: 1.25m (4ft 1in)
Weight in running order: 84 tonnes
UIC power rating: 4,000kW (5,375hp)
Maximum speed:
7201-35/7343-80/7411-40 100km/h (62mph)
7236-7344/7381-7410 160km/h (99mph)
Pantograph type: AM18B single arm
Nominal supply voltage: 1,500V dc
Depots of allocation:
100km/h: LI, CY
160km/h: PS, VE
Works responsible: Oullins
Livery: Silver-grey with orange flash and dark grey round windows

With the very similar ac locomotives of Class BB 15000 and the dual current Class BB 22200, this is SNCF's standard mixed traffic locomotive of the 1970s & 1980s. Production of these three classes will very soon finish and give way to a new standard electric design which will begin with BB 26000. Throughout the class, locomotives are almost identical except in details which are difficult or impossible to see.

The first batch, BB 7201-35, were built with high speed bogies but later received 100km/h bogies in order to work heavy freight on the Sud Ouest region. For this, they are based at LI. The only physical difference between them and later members of the class is their windscreen, which is slightly less slanted than the others. Unlike later 100km/h members, they are not fitted for multiple working. The photograph shows BB 7206 hauling a freight at Villeneuve Saint Georges.

The majority of the class, BB 7236-BB 7342 and BB 7381-BB 7410, are fitted with higher geared bogies and are used as mixed traffic locomotives. They work most of the fastest non-TGV passenger trains on the Sud Est region and an increasing number over the Sud Ouest, as units are transferred from VE to PS depot. They also haul a large amount of freight traffic on both regions. In the photograph above, BB 7271 is seen passing south through Villeneuve St Georges.

The batches BB 7343-BB 7380 and BB 7411-BB 7440 are allocated to Chambéry for working freight, particularly on the 'Maurienne' route (see CC 6500). Their diagram includes workings singly as far as Paris, but the majority of their work is east of Chambéry, especially between St Jean de Maurienne and Modane. There, they are used in pairs to bank eastbound freights or to add extra brake force to westbound ones. For this work they are fitted with 100km/h bogies, with jumper cables for multiple working and with special brake blocks. The latest batch, although outwardly identical to the others, contain several improvements to the original design including regenerative brakes and the first control microchips to be used in SNCF locomotives. As such they will serve as testbeds for future developments for use in Class BB 26000 and the TGV-Atlantique. In the third view, two of the earlier batch, BB 7371 and BB 7368 leave Modane with a freight from Italy. The jumper cable, which is not present on earlier locomotives, can just be seen on the far left of the buffer beam.

Classes BB 8000 and BB 8100

Number series: BB 8001
BB 8101-BB 8271 (171)
Former numbers: SNCF 0401 (BB 8001)
Built by:
Alsthom 8001, 8101-19/8134-89
Schneider Jeumont/SW 8120-28/
8190-8225
Compagnie Générale de Construction
de Locomotives/Oerlikon 8129-33/
8226-71
Introduced: 1947-55
Type: Bo-Bo
Length: 12.93m (42ft 5in)
Wheelbase: 8.95m (29ft 4in)
Wheel diameter: 1.4m (4ft 7in)
Weight in running order: 92 tonnes
UIC power rating: 1,760kW (2,360hp)
Maximum speed: 105km/h (65mph)
Pantograph type: Faiveley G diamond
Nominal supply voltage: 1,500V dc
Depots of allocation: AN, DN
Works responsible: Béziers
Livery: Dark green with red buffer beams and bodyside window frames. Now appearing in pale grey lined in orange

These short, austere-looking electrics were developed from Class BB 300 and are extremely robust and reliable. They are therefore to be found on freight duties everywhere on the Sud Est dc network, except between Béziers and Neussargues, as well as on the southern part of the Sud Ouest region. BB 8001, which served as the prototype for the class, is identical to the rest. The photograph shows BB 8141 running light through Lyon Perrache station. They can be identified simply as the only small, plain dark green electrics with two front windows at work on long distance freight now that the second batch of Class BB 300 have been declassified. The small snowploughs seen here are not common, and will probably be removed as the class leaves Chambéry depot. Dutch Railways (NS) bought 60 locomotives of a very similar design: their Class 1100, which have now been fitted with reinforced noses.

Class BB 8500

Number series: BB 8501-BB 8646 (146)
Built by: Alsthom
Introduced: 1964-74
Type: B-B
Length:
8501-8536 14.7m (48ft 3in)
8537-8587 14.94m (49ft 0in)
8588-8646 15.57m (51ft 1in)
Wheelbase: 10.108m (33ft 2in)
Wheel diameter: 1.1m (3ft 7in)
Weight in running order: 79 tonnes
UIC power rating:
8501-8511 2,610kW (3,500hp)
8512-8646 2,940kW (3,950hp)
Maximum speed:
PV 90km/h (56mph)
GV 140km/h (87mph)
Pantograph type: AM18B single arm
Nominal supply voltage: 1,500V dc
Depots of allocation: LA, VE, TE, MR
Works responsible: Béziers
Livery: Blue/green lined in white with dark grey round windows (and dark green panel round upper grilles on early locomotives) and see below

BB 8500 is one of three standard mixed traffic electric classes built in the late 1960s and early 1970s, and is very similar externally to the equivalent 25kV ac design BB 17000 and dual current BB 25500. Although virtually identical, it is impossible to confuse BB 8500 and BB 17000 as their areas of action are mutually exclusive. However, it is possible to see both BB 8500 and BB 25500 locomotives in many places, especially to the south of Paris towards Orléans and Tours. The most obvious way of distinguishing a BB 8500 locomotive is by the small box mounted just forward of the pantograph on the cab roof, a feature which does not exist on BB 25500. Several detail differences exist between batches within Class BB 8500, the most significant of which are the lateral grilles, cab design and buffer beam. The first batch, BB 8501-8536, have small recessed lateral grilles grouped in pairs and a buffer beam flush with the cab front. Certain members may have a lateral white line which continues round the front of the locomotive. But in this view of No BB 8527 on Paris Sud Ouest depot, the line is restricted to the side.

The second distinct batch, BB 8537-8567, differ from the first group in being slightly longer because they have a reinforced buffer beam which can be seen to project slightly from the cab front. Within this group, locomotives up to No BB 8548 were built with cast numbers and letters on their sides whilst those from BB 8549 on have yellow stickers. However, this distinction is disappearing as some earlier locomotives, such as No BB 8537, seen here with a freight at Juvisy, and BB 8527 in the previous photograph, are appearing with yellow stickers too. The majority of the first two batches are allocated to LA depot from which they work mainly freight. VE and MR locomotives, on the other hand are mainly engaged on suburban passenger duties out of Montparnasse and Paris Lyon.

The next modification to be made was to BB 8568-8587 which have longer, oblong grilles which project a little from the sides of the locomotives.

The final modification brought the greatest change in appearance. First, the chassis was lengthened in order to allow the locomotives to be fitted with UIC automatic couplers. This had the added benefit of giving the driver a more spacious cab. In addition, the small side grilles were replaced by one large one on each side, to improve ventilation. Almost all this final batch are allocated to Toulouse from where they haul both freight and passenger services, sometimes triple-headed, over the steeply graded lines in the Pyrenees. This view shows BB 8606 and BB 8629 at La Tour de Carol, on the Spanish frontier, with a passenger train for Paris. The whole class is now appearing in pale grey and orange like Class BB 17000.

Class 2D2 9100

Number series: 2D2 9101-2D2 9135 (11)
Built by: Fives Lille/CEM
Introduced: 1950-51
Type: 2Do2
Length: 18.08m (59ft 4in)
Wheelbase: 14.69m (48ft 2in)
Driving wheel diameter: 1.75m (5ft 9in)
Pony wheel diameter: 1.0m (3ft 4in)
Weight in working order: 144 tonnes
UIC power rating: 3,690kW (4,950hp)
Maximum speed: 140km/h (87mph)
Pantograph type: Faiveley G diamond
Nominal supply voltage: 1,500V dc
Depot of allocation: LN
Works responsible: No longer overhauled
Livery: Green with red buffer beams and aluminium trim

These unusual machines are the last of a string of 2D2 designs which have served on SNCF's 1,500V dc network. With their deep frontal 'V' and wheel arrangement they are easily identified, but, unfortunately, by the time this book appears, very few are likely to remain in regular service. A small number may be dusted off at peak times such as in the winter sports or summer holiday seasons when other, more modern locomotives are in demand for extra passenger trains. Their normal duties remain haulage of freight on the 'classic' Paris-Dijon-Lyon-Marseille line and so they may still turn up at Villeneuve or Juvisy from time to time. Here, 2D2 9126 runs into the roundhouse at its home depot, Lyon Mouche.

Class BB 9200

Number series: BB 9201-BB 9292 (91)
Built by: Schneider Jeumont/CEM
Introduced: 1957-64
Type: Bo-Bo
Length: 16.2m (53ft 2in)
Wheelbase: 12.4m (40ft 8in)
Wheel diameter: 1.25m (4ft 1in)
Weight in working order: 80-83 tonnes
UIC power rating: 3,850kW (5,170hp)
Maximum speed: 160km/h (99mph)
Pantograph type: Faiveley G diamond
Nominal supply voltage: 1,500V dc
Depots of allocation: BX, PS
Works responsible: Oullins
Livery: Blue/green with aluminium flashes or lined in off white. Dark grey round windows. Other liveries – see below

Class BB 9200 is one of the standard SNCF express passenger designs of the late 1950s and early 1960s, along with the 25kV ac version BB 16000 and the dual current versions BB 25100, BB 25150 and BB 25200. These designs are all very similar, but Class BB 9200 is easy to distinguish as it is the only one of the group with diamond pantographs and lateral grilles which are restricted to the central sections of the body sides. Although still used for passenger duties throughout the Sud Ouest region, they lost the fastest trains to Class CC 6500 some years ago and their duties now include as many freight as passenger turns. The remarkable point about this class is the number of different liveries – six different at present – making it the most colourful class of locomotives in France. Locomotives were originally built in plain blue/green enlivened by aluminium 'moustaches' and headlight fairings. Perhaps a third of the class remain like this, including BB 9258 seen here on Paris Sud Ouest depot.

Because the aluminium trim was found to corrode severely, a new 'standard' livery was adopted in the mid-1970s and now about half the class are painted like this. A slightly different tone of blue/green was adopted relieved by white 'moustaches', containing the number, on the front ends and a broad white lateral stripe at headlight level. Cast numerals and letters have been replaced by yellow stickers. BB 9275 is seen like this on a passenger working at Saint Pierre des Corps (Tours).

In 1981, BB 9231 and BB 9288 received an experimental livery designed by SNCF's house designer, Paul Arzens, who is responsible for many of the designs at present to be seen. Although these colour schemes are not to be adopted generally, and will probably disappear when the locomotives next are overhauled, a similar livery has been adopted as standard for Class BB 9400. Both locomotives are silver-grey with dark grey roof, underframe and round cab windows, with yellow triangles on the front ends, yellow letters and numerals and a red patch on the buffer beam. The other dominant colour, which covers the lateral grilles and forms a frontal 'moustache' and lateral stripes, is dark green on No BB 9231 and dark grey on BB 9288. The success of the final result can be judged on BB 9288, standing on Paris Sud Ouest depot. Note that this locomotive is fitted for push-pull working.

In 1978, BB 9280/1/2/8/91/2 were modified to work push-pull rakes of Corail stock on the Paris-Poitiers route, where reversals are necessary at both Tours and Orléans. For this they have a group of jumper cable sockets built under the right hand headlight. These locomotives were repainted in 'Corail' colours of dark grey, with an orange lateral band at headlight level and pale grey below that and at roof level. Of these six, BB 9280/8 have further been repainted (see other photographs). Of the remaining four, BB 9281/91 have retained their original aluminium trim, whilst BB 9282/92 have lost it and have a pale grey 'moustache' and 'SNCF' in yellow letters on the front ends. These two versions can be compared on BB 9281 and BB 9292, both photographed on Paris Sud Ouest depot.

As if that wasn't colourful enough, SNCF decided, in late 1984, to adopt a new standard livery, like that applied for some years to Class BB 17000. BB 9280 *Arpajon* was the first locomotive to be repainted and is seen here at Les Aubrais (Orléans) with a train for Vierzon. It is pale grey with an orange 'moustache' and lateral band at buffer beam level and dark grey grilles and around the cab windows. All members of the class should appear in this livery as they are overhauled.

Class BB 9300

Number series: BB 9301-BB 9340 (40)
Built by: Schneider/MTE/CEM
Introduced: 1967-69
Type: Bo-Bo
Length: 16.2m (53ft 2in)
Wheelbase: 12.4m (40ft 8in)
Wheel diameter: 1.25m (4ft 1in)
Weight in running order: 82 tonnes
UIC power rating: 3,850kW (5,170hp)
Maximum speed: 160km/h (99mph)
Pantograph type: AM18B single arm
Nominal supply voltage: 1,500V dc
Depots of allocation: TE
Works responsible: Oullins
Livery: Blue/green with off-white body stripe and 'moustaches' and yellow and white SNCF roundel. Dark grey around cab windows. Appearing in pale grey lined in orange as per BB 9280

This class is very similar in design and performance to Class BB 9200 but includes several technical improvements. In particular, all units have rheostatic brakes and single arm pantographs which distinguish them visibly from the BB 9200s. Other visual points of distinction are the longer lateral grilles. Most locomotives also have a circular SNCF symbol, deeper 'moustaches' and lower number position on the nose although No BB 9302 appeared in the same livery as BB 9275 (see page 31) early in 1985. Now, pale grey and orange has been adopted as standard for the class. Although all are allocated to Toulouse depot, they can be seen all over the Sud Ouest network as well as in Avignon and Marseille. Like Class BB 9200 they work a mixture of passenger and freight duties. Here, BB 9320 runs light through Bordeaux St Jean station.

Class BB 9400

Number series: BB 9401-BB 9535 (130)
Built by: Fives-Lille-Cail/MTE/CEM
Introduced: 1960-64
Type: B-B
Length: 14.4m (47ft 3in)
Wheelbase: 10.4m (34ft 1in)
Wheel diameter: 1.02m (3ft 4in)
Weight in running order: 64 tonnes
UIC power rating: 2,210kW (2,970hp)
Maximum speed: 130km/h (81mph)
Pantograph type: AM14 single arm
Nominal supply voltage: 1,500V dc
Depots of allocation: BX, LN, AN
Works responsible: Béziers
Livery: Blue/green with aluminium trim and off white body strips (also see below)

The members of Class BB 9400 are light, medium powered mixed traffic locomotives which are used mainly in the area south of Lyon and Bordeaux, having few duties which take them north to Paris. Their main duties are on freight, on which they are frequently used in multiple, their only regular passenger duties being on the mountainous Béziers-Neussargues line. In their original state they are not dissimilar to Class BB 9200 but can be distinguished by their smaller size, single arm pantographs, jumper cables on the nose and the unusual shields for the bogie suspension. The class was built in two batches, the main difference being that BB 9401-9435 have raised 'humps' on the roof to support the pantographs whereas BB 9436-9535 have a flat roof with the pantographs mounted on pillars. The difference can be seen clearly on the photographs of BB 9426 and BB 9449.

All locomotives of this class were originally built in blue/green with aluminium 'moustaches' and headlight fairings like BB 9503 seen here at Lyon Part Dieu with a supplementary passenger train in the ski season.

Like Class BB 9200, it was found that the aluminium trim corroded badly and so a new livery of blue/green with white 'moustaches' and lateral bands at headlight level and yellow sticker numerals and letters was adopted. Several locomotives have retained their cast letters and numbers, like No BB 9453, seen below passing Bordeaux depot.

In the mid-1970s another new livery, of silver-grey with chocolate brown front ends, lateral stripes and grilles, and yellow frontal triangle, numbers and letters, became standard for the class. All locomotives will receive this livery as they pass through works. BB 9513 is seen opposite in a very clean condition on Villeneuve depot.

Classs BB 12000

Number series: BB 12001-BB 12148 (145)
Built by:
12001-34/65-148 MTE/SW
12035-64 Alsthom/SW
Introduced: 1954-1961
Type: Bo-Bo
Length: 15.2m (49ft 10in)
Wheelbase: 11.4m (37ft 5in)
Wheel diameter: 1.25m (4ft 1in)
Weight in running order: 82-86 tonnes
UIC power rating: 2,470kW (3,320hp)
Maximum speed: 120km/h (75mph)
Pantograph type: Faiveley MT diamond
Nominal supply voltage: 25kV ac 50Hz
Depots of allocation: MN, LO, TV
Works responsible: Epernay
Livery: Dark green with yellow nose panel and red buffer beams

Although built as mixed traffic engines for the electrification of the Nord and Est regions, Class BB 12000 lost most of its passenger duties with the arrival of Classes BB 15000 and BB 16000. They now haul very few passenger trains, except for a few peak hour extras on the Est region. However, on freight they can be seen virtually anywhere on these two regions, from Dunkerque to Luxembourg, Basle and Paris, as well as on the Ouest region on trains to Rouen and Le Havre. The class can easily be recognised by its distinctive centre cab outline, which provokes the nicknames 'boîte à sel' – salt box and 'fer à repasser' – flat iron, although it is difficult to tell the difference between this class and BB 13000 which can be seen side by side, particularly around Metz, Strasbourg and Nancy. Minor technical differences exist between different members of the class and there are small external differences in the arrangement of grilles. In general, earlier locomotives have two small lumps on the nose where there were once tail lights, like Classes BB 13000 and CC 14100, but later models, like BB 12129 seen here with a freight at Lens, have no lumps.

Class BB 13000

Number series: BB 13001-BB 13053 (43)
Built by:
13001-15 MTE/Jeumont
13016-24 Fives Lille/Jeumont
13025-36 SLM/Oerlikon
13037-44 SLM/Brown Boveri
13045-49 SLM/Ateliers Sécheron
13050-53 Fives Lille/Jeumont
Introduced: 1954-57
Type: Bo-Bo
Length: 15.2m (49ft 10in)
Wheelbase: 11.4m (37ft 5in)
Wheel diameter: 1.25m (4ft 1in)
Weight in running order: 84 tonnes
UIC power rating:
13001-13015 2,000kW (2,690hp)
13016-13053 2,130kW (2,860hp)
Maximum speed:
13001-13015 105km/h (65mph)
13016-13053 120km/h (75mph)
Pantograph type: Faiveley MT diamond
Nominal supply voltage: 25kV ac 50Hz
Depot of allocation: SG
Works responsible: No longer overhauled
Livery: Dark green with yellow nose panel and red buffer beams

Class BB 13000 is very similar to BB 12000 externally, but differs in certain technical details, especially in techniques of current rectification. There are no very clear ways of telling these two classes apart at a distance. The class was built in two batches, the first of which, BB 13001-15, have a lower power rating and maximum speed. Few of this group remain in service and their duties limit them to freight in the Strasbourg and Nancy areas. The second batch is also being withdrawn due to a decline in freight traffic in the industrial area of Lorraine. Those which remain work over most of the Est region, especially around Nancy, principally on freight, but also on a few passenger duties. The class were once common in Lille, but are now quite rare. However, BB 13046 was caught on camera there in early 1985.

Class CC 14100

Number series: CC 14101-CC 14202 (75)
Built by:
Alsthom/Fives-Lille/CEM
Introduced: 1954-1958
Type: Co-Co
Length: 18.89m (62ft 0in)
Wheelbase: 14.10m (4[illegible]ft [illegible]in)
Wheel diameter: 1.1m (3ft 7in)
Weight in running order: 127 tonnes
UIC power rating: 2,600kW (3,490hp)
Maximum speed: 60km/h (37mph)
Pantograph type: Faiveley MT diamond
Nominal supply voltage: 25kV ac 50Hz
Depots of allocation: MN, TV
Works responsible: No longer overhauled
Livery: Dark green with yellow nose panel and red buffer beams

As can be deduced from its maximum speed, this is a class built for heavy freight haulage, and conceived for the electrification of the Metz-Lille-Dunkerque corridor, which is an important freight route but has little passenger traffic. Despite being withdrawn gradually, due to the recession in heavy industry, they can still be seen in large numbers on this route and its branches, but rarely elsewhere. Their length gives them an impressive look and they can be distinguished easily from the previous two centre cab designs by their sloping footplate and larger bogies. Here CC 14109 is seen on the stabling point at Lille (La Délivrance) marshalling yard.

Class BB 15000 (& BB 10003/4)

Number series: BB 15001-BB 15065 (61)
Built by: Alsthom/MTE
Introduced: 1971-78
Type: B-B
Length: 17.48m (57ft 4in)
Wheelbase: 12.494m (41ft 0in)
Wheel diameter: 1.25m (4ft 1in)
Weight in running order: 87-90 tonnes
UIC power rating: 4,620kW (6,200hp)
Maximum speed: 160km/h (99mph)
Pantograph type: AM18U1 single arm
Nominal supply voltage: 25kV ac 50Hz
Depot of allocation: SG
Works responsible: Hellemmes
Livery: Silver-grey with red panels on sides and noses lined in orange. Dark grey round cab windows

Class BB 15000 was the first of a new generation of electric locomotives for the 1970s from which were developed Classes BB 7200 and BB 22200. A total of over 450 units of these three classes have been built. This group is now complete and will be, in future, superseded by all-purpose, synchronous motored locomotives starting with Class BB 26000. Class BB 15000 are unique in having the same sized body as Classes BB 7200 and BB 22200 but with a different livery – the same 'Trans Europ Express' colours as Class CC 6500. Confusion with any of these classes is therefore difficult. The class has a well defined operating area, having the monopoly of express passenger trains over electrified lines on the Est region. On certain trains, locomotives of this class start and finish their turn outside France, as they work both to Luxemburg and to Basle in Switzerland. The class was built in three distinct batches. The first, Nos BB 15001-15, can be recognised by their deep lateral grilles offset from the centre of the body side. The first five of the class originally ran in a plain green livery similar to that carried by the 'Maurienne' CC 6500s. Now all have been repainted in the standard livery. The photograph below shows BB 15004 on La Villette depot, in front of two BB 15000 locomotives from the second batch.

The main batch, BB 15016-50, has slightly shallower lateral grilles, set off-centre, in stainless steel. Although the class works almost entirely on the Est region, locomotives had a regular turn to Lille until recently. No BB 15044 is seen there having returned from Paris Nord.

The final batch, BB 15051-65, has a body very similar to Classes BB 7200 and BB 22200, with a central grille panel and the more modern, rectangular SNCF symbol on the nose in place of the previous roundel. The illustration below shows No BB 15051 having just arrived at its 'home' town of Strasbourg with a morning train from Paris which conveys a motorail portion.

Class BB 15000 has a long history of being used for tests of new equipment or as prototypes for new classes. A crucial factor in this choice is the proximity to Strasbourg, their home depot, of the Belfort factory of Alsthom-Atlantique, which is the company most responsible for technical developments in the SNCF fleet. Another important point is that there exists between Strasbourg and Mulhouse, a stretch of line in the Rhine valley which is perfect for use as a high speed test track. At present, at least six members of the class are fitted with non-standard equipment. BB 15020-24 have experimental simplified pantographs, and BB 15063, which can be seen in the photograph has specially adapted bogies with modified suspension.

It will be noticed from the total number of the class in service that four locomotives are 'missing'. Nos BB 15011 and BB 15057 were both withdrawn after serious accidents but the other two have been converted for experimental use. BB 15007 was first converted, in the 1970s, into BB 7003 which was a 1,500V dc locomotive which served as a prototype for Class BB 7200. After several years of tests which resulted in the production of over 200 of this class, No BB 7003 disappeared from the scene and spent a long period in Alsthom's Belfort workshops being further modified. It has now reappeared as BB 10003, once again an ac locomotive, but with very different characteristics to Class BB 15000. It has retained the same general outline (unfortunately, no photograph is available as it spends the majority of its time in the workshops), but has a livery similar to Classes BB 7200 and BB 22200 with the addition of a red band at headlight level. Other differences are that it has a lower bodyside grille, similar to that on Class BB 7200 but split into two parts and separated by an access door in the middle of the body. It also has completely different bogies which house asynchronous motors powering each axle (BB 15000 bogies are monomotor). SNCF's experimentation with asynchronous motors is a further step in their search for a 'universal' electric locomotive, and can be compared to DB's (German Railways) research based on their Class 120.

More can be written about BB 10004 which was converted from BB 15055. This locomotive has been SNCF's testbed for synchronous motors which are to be used in Class BB 26000, whose full production will begin in mid-1986. BB 10004 looks similar to a standard Class BB 15000 except that it has dark blue instead of red panels on its fronts and sides. It has now finished tests and disappeared back into Alsthom's works at Belfort. Further tests with synchronous motors are to be made with prototypes BB 20011/12 (see Class BB 22200 notes) before BB 26000 production begins, and with a pair of TGV power cars in order to develop synchronous motors for the TGV-Atlantique. These results so far have been so successful that SNCF believe that the conventional dc traction motor is doomed, and that the future lies with this development of the three-phase motor. Three targets were set for BB 10004, which is rated at 5,600kW (7,500hp): haulage of the longest SNCF passenger trains (16 Corail coaches) at 200km/h, haulage of freight trains of 2,050 tonnes up banks of 1 in 113 at 80km/h without overheating and various adhesion targets. All this, without passing a weight limit of 90 tonnes per locomotive. Although final tests are still to be made, SNCF is now past the mock-up stage of producing Class BB 26000. These locomotives will break with the tradition of the past 15 years in changing the 'swept-back' front end design of BB 15000 and others for a more streamlined look, with fairings to reduce pantograph drag together with smoother noses and sides. Engines are likely to appear in a variation of the TGV orange, dark grey and white.

Class BB 16000

Number series: BB 16001-BB 16062 (60)
Built by: MTE
Introduced: 1958-63
Type: Bo-Bo
Length: 16.2m (53ft 2in)
Wheelbase: 12.4m (40ft 8in)
Wheel diameter: 1.25m (4ft 1in)
Weight in running order: 88 tonnes
UIC power rating: 4,130kW (5,540hp)
Maximum speed: 160km/h (99mph)
Pantograph type: AM11 single arm
Nominal supply voltage: 25kV ac 50Hz
Depot of allocation: LF
Works responsible: Hellemmes
Livery: Blue/green with aluminium trim and dark grey round cab windows. Now appearing in pale grey lined in orange as per BB 9280

Class BB 16000 is the ac equivalent of BB 9200 and is similar in design. It is unlikely to be confused with the latter as they work under different voltages and because of physical differences in appearance. Although Classes BB 25100 and BB 25150 are also similar they do not share the same territory. Only examples of Class BB 25200 are likely to be seen side by side with BB 16000 and even then, only occasionally. The main outward difference between these two classes is in their buffer beams. BB 16000 have a protruding, reinforced cross head, whereas BB 25200 have a 'skirt' flush with the body front, as did BB 16000 originally. BB 16000 is now the standard passenger engine for electrified lines in the Nord region but also has some freight duties and works on the St Lazare-Le Havre route. Here, BB 16035 is seen at Jeumont on the French/Belgian border just before being uncoupled from the 16.20 Paris-Moscow (!) via Liège, Cologne and Warsaw.

Class BB 16000 were originally fitted with single anode (ignitron) rectifiers. BB 16012 was then fitted experimentally with silicon rectifiers, and, as can be seen from this photograph taken at La Chapelle depot, can be distinguished by the additional grilles in its sides. Now all locomotives of the class have been fitted with silicon rectifiers but it has not been thought necessary to provide the extra grilles.

Nos BB 16003/6/7/8/18/32/9/44/7/53 are fitted with similar equipment to certain locomotives of Class BB 9200 for push-pull working Corail stock on the Paris St Lazare-Le Havre line. Like corresponding members of Class BB 9200, they have a group of jumper cable connections built in a box on the bottom right of the front end (with four connections against the three of Class BB 9200) and are painted in 'Corail' dark and light grey lined in orange. Although mainly used on the Le Havre route, they also appear on other BB 16000 duties, like No BB 16039 seen on Lille (Fives) depot.

Class BB 16500

Number series: BB 16501-BB 16794 (294)
Built by: Alsthom
Introduced: 1958-64
Type: B-B
Length: 14.4m (47ft 0in) except 16700 15.[illegible]m (50ft [illegible]in)
Wheelbase: 9.808m (32ft 2in)
Wheel diameter: 1.1m (3ft 7in)
Weight in running order: 71-74 tonnes except No 16700: 81 tonnes
UIC power rating: 2,580kW (3,465hp)
Maximum speed:
PV 90km/h (56mph)
GV 140km/h (87mph)
Pantograph type: AM11 single arm
Nominal supply voltage: 25kV ac 50Hz
Depots of allocation: LS, LV
Works responsible: Epernay
Livery: Blue/green lined in white with dark green panel round upper grilles and dark grey round cab windows and red buffer beam (also see below)

Class BB 16500 was the first of a series of medium powered, mixed traffic electrics with an unattractive 'box-on-wheels' outline which was continued with Classes BB 8500, BB 17000 and BB 25500. Although having very similar front ends to the latter classes, BB 16500s can be distinguished by their different arrangement of lateral grilles and a bodyside which drops lower between the bogies where the other classes have a straight base line. Although the 294 members of the class are allocated to only Lens and Paris La Villette depots, they can be found anywhere on the Nord and Est electrified networks as well as on trains to Rouen and Le Havre on the Ouest region. Their workings include freight both singly and in multiple, a small number of express passenger trains over short distances, and a large number of push-pull suburban passenger trains, particularly out of Paris Est, around Lille and Strasbourg, and on the Thionville-Nancy corridor. Only one significant visible difference exists between individual members of the class, that is in the pattern of lateral air vents. The majority of the class have four main blocks of vents which protrude from the body side, as seen here on No BB 16604 at Chelles in the eastern Paris suburbs. No BB 16604 also has an experimental livery of chocolate brown relieved by silver-grey vertical and horizontal panels, and a yellow frontal triangle. BB 16789 has a similar livery based on dark green. These liveries were again designed by Paul Arzens (see Class BB 9200), perhaps to try to improve the appearance of these ugly beasts. This livery will not be applied to other members of the class as a pale grey livery has been chosen as standard.

A smaller number of locomotives, particularly those in the last 50, have a group of grilles along the top of the bodyside which do not protrude. It is probable that these will be modified on passage through works. Here No BB 16539 is seen at Lille with a local train for Hazebrouck.

BB 16700, which is pictured here at Metz depot, has a strange outline, with 'false noses', because it was experimentally modified, with reinforced front ends to receive UIC automatic couplings. Although the experiment has not been followed up, the locomotive remains fitted with an automatic coupling at one end and is permanently coupled to the match wagon seen in the photograph. The locomotive has a special diagram and works a daily return freight between the yards at Metz and Vaires (in the eastern Paris suburbs), places where it can easily be turned.

Early in 1985 locomotives passing through works started to be repainted in pale grey lined in orange which is also being applied to several other classes. Apart from the colours already mentioned, the area around the cab windows and upper grilles is dark grey. The cast numerals on the side have been replaced by dark grey transfers.

Class BB 17000

Number series: BB 17001-BB 17105 (105)
Built by: Alsthom
Introduced: 1965-68
Type: B-B
Length:
17001-[illegible] (48ft 3in)
17005 15.57m (51ft 1in)
17038-105 14.94m (49ft 0in)
Wheelbase: 10.108m (33ft 2in)
Wheel diameter: 1.1m (3ft 7in)
Weight in running order: 78 tonnes
UIC power rating: 2,940kW (3,950hp)
Maximum speed:
PV 90km/h (56mph)
GV 140km/h (87mph)
Pantograph type: [illegible] single arm
Nominal supply voltage: 25kV ac 50Hz
Depots of allocation: AS, LE
Works responsible: Hellemmes
Livery: Pale grey lined in orange with dark grey round cab windows and round upper body grilles (also see below)

This class is the ac equivalent of the BB 8500 but has very different duties. Although they haul a few freight trains, particularly on the Paris-Le Havre route, BB 17000 locomotives are mainly used on suburban passenger trains out of Paris Nord and St Lazare. There is thus little chance of confusing the two classes as they are not likely to be seen in the same place. However, there is no easy way of telling early members of Class BB 25500 and BB 17000 apart if both are in the same livery. There exist slight differences in body length between the two batches of Class BB 17000, corresponding to the first two batches of class BB 8500 – the first batch has buffer beams flush with the front end, the second having a projecting buffer beam. The only other variation is BB 17005, which has an outline not unlike No BB 16700. In 1975, the locomotive was involved in an accident and was rebuilt on a longer chassis, like that of the last members of Classes BB 8500 and BB 25500. This meant building up a 'nose' at both ends in order to make good the difference in chassis and body lengths. The photograph, however, illustrates a standard member of the class in grey livery – BB 17099 at Paris Nord.

Class BB 20200

Number series: BB 20201-BB 20213 (13)
Built by: Alsthom
Introduced: 1970
Type: B-B
Length: 14.94m (49ft 0in)
Wheelbase: 10.108m (33ft 2in)
Wheel diameter: 1.1m (3ft 7in)
Weight in running order: 80 tonnes
UIC power rating:
Under 15kV 1,660kW (2,220hp)
Under 25kV 2,940kW (3,950hp)

Maximum speed:
PV 90km/h (56mph)
GV 140km/h (87mph)
Pantograph type: AM18U single arm
Nominal supply voltages:
France 25kV ac 50Hz
Switzerland/Germany 15kV ac 16⅔Hz
Depot of allocation: SG
Works responsible: Hellemmes
Livery: Blue/green lined in white with dark green panel round upper grilles and dark grey round cab windows. Now appearing in pale grey lined in orange as per Class BB 17000

This class is a version of Class BB 17000 which can work at reduced power on the German and Swiss 15kV ac systems. Although having the same outline as Classes BB 8500, BB 17000 and BB 25500, locomotives of this class can be recognised immediately by the headlight fitted on top of the cab which is obligatory for working in Germany and Switzerland. The main duties of the class are freights between the Strasbourg area and St Louis and Muttenz yards in Basle, although they also work odd trains the short distance between Strasbourg and Kehl (Germany). The photograph shows No BB 20202 running light onto Strasbourg depot.

Class CC 21000

Number series: CC 21001-CC 21004 (4)
Built by: Alsthom/MTE
Introduced: 21001/2 1969
21003/4 1974
Type: C-C
Length: 20.19m (66ft 3in)
Wheelbase: [illegible] (4?ft 11in)
Wheel diameter: 1.12m (3ft 8in)
Weight in running order: 125-128 tonnes
UIC power rating: 5,760kW (7,740hp)

Maximum speed:
PV 100km/h (62mph)
GV 200km/h (124mph)
Pantograph type:
dc AM18B single arm
ac AM18U single arm
Nominal supply voltages:
1,500V dc
25kV ac 50Hz
Depot of allocation: DN
Works responsible: Oullins
Livery: Silver-grey with red panels on sides and noses lined in orange. Dark grey round cab windows

This class is a dual current version of Class CC 6500 built for work on express passenger trains between Paris and Lausanne as far as the French frontier at Vallorbe. As such, they have recently been replaced by TGVs and, with competition from the more modern Class BB 22200, they are often missing from their regular diagram. Due to their non-standard design and high maintenance costs, they have an uncertain future. Built in two batches of two, some time apart, they are very similar to the first and last batches of Class CC 6500, the first two having horizontal 'slat' type grilles which harmonize well with the overall body design whilst the second two have a large rectangular grille, offset from the centre of the body side. They can be distinguished from their dc only equivalents by their extra pantograph and by the large equipment block between the bogies where CC 6500 have a small box on one side and an air brake reservoir on the other. No CC 21002 is seen at Paris Gare de Lyon. Also visible on the end are cable sockets used when hauling test trains on the 'Ligne à Grande Vitesse'. Both CC 21001 and this locomotive are fitted for working on the high speed line.

Class BB 22200 (& BB 20011/2)

Number series: BB 22201-BB 22405 (202)
Built by: Alsthom/MTE
Introduced: 1976-86
Type: B-B
Length: 17.48m (57ft 4in)
Wheelbase: 12.494m (41ft 0in)
Wheel diameter: 1.25m (4ft 1in)
Weight in running order: 89 tonnes
UIC power rating: 4,000kW (5,375hp)
Maximum speed:
22201-77/80-350/61-405 160km/h (99mph)
22278, 22351-60 200km/h (124mph)
Pantograph type:
dc AM18B single arm
ac AM18U single arm
Nominal supply voltages:
1,500V dc
25kV ac 50Hz
Depots of allocation: DN, ME, RS
Works responsible: Oullins
Livery: Silver-grey with orange flash and dark grey round windows

BB 22200 are the dual-current equivalents of Classes BB 7200 and BB 15000, and are truly all-purpose units, being able to work anywhere on SNCF's electrified network on most sorts of traffic. Although having an identical body and livery to Class BB 7200, they can be identified by their pantographs which lie in the same direction, whereas those on BB 7200 are fitted to face in opposite directions. The difference can be seen in the photograph of Nos BB 22220 and BB 7277, which shows how the BB 22200 pantograph overhangs the cab roof whilst the BB 7200 pantograph is set back from the front of the locomotive.

Although Class BB 22200 can be seen over much of the Sud Est network, their main duties are, for Marseille units, trains on the Côte D'Azur from Marseille to Ventimiglia in Italy, and for Dijon locomotives, trains which cross the 1,500V dc/25kV ac divide towards Besançon and Frasne to the east of Dijon and on long distance express freights between the Sud Est and other regions. For instance, one locomotive stays at the head of a freight from Avignon to Lille, a run of well over 600 miles. Locomotives which work to Lille are then used on passenger trains to Paris Nord and return. Seen above at Douai is BB 22301 *Villeneuve D'Ascq* with a Paris-Lille train which includes a car transporter wagon from Nice. The 20 units of the class allocated to Rennes are more restricted in their range, only working passenger trains from Paris Montparnasse to Rennes and Nantes. Ten of them, BB 22351-60, can operate at 200km/h instead of the usual 160 and for this are fitted with 'préannonce' cab signalling and a special pantograph which has a small aileron to maintain wire contact. This can clearly be seen in the photograph below. This batch was developed after No BB 22278 was used as a 200km/h prototype. They work, in particular, to Nantes as it is the Le Mans-Nantes line which is suitable for 200km/h running. One of the lower speed locomotives, BB 22366 *Malakoff* is pictured below at Rennes. After BB 22278, two further engines, Nos BB 22379/80, were converted in 1985 to serve as prototypes for 'Sybic' (*Sy*nchronous motors, *Bi*-current) locomotives of Class BB 26000. As such, they are numbered BB 20011/12 – and carry a special livery of silver grey lined out in orange and dark blue.

Class BB 25100

Number series: BB 25101-BB 25125 (25)
Built by: MTE
Introduced: 1964-65
Type: Bo-Bo
Length: 16.2m (53ft 2in)
Wheelbase: 12.4m (40ft 8in)
Wheel diameter: 1.25m (4ft 1in)
Weight in running order: 85 tonnes
UIC power rating:
Under 1,500V dc 3,400kW (4,560hp)
Under 25kV ac 4,130kW (5,540hp)
Maximum speed: 130km/h (81mph)
Pantograph type:
dc AM18B single arm
ac AM18U single arm
Nominal supply voltages:
1,500V dc
25kV ac 50Hz
Depot of allocation: CH
Works responsible: Hellemmes
Livery: Blue/green with aluminium trim and dark grey round cab windows. Now appearing in pale grey lined in orange as per BB 9280

Class BB 25100 were the first dual current express passenger locomotives built for SNCF and were developed from Class BB 16000 which they closely resemble. They can be distinguished from that class, however, by their valanced buffer beam which is replaced by a protruding cross beam on the BB 16000s. They are also seen in a completely different area of France, having an almost total monopoly of the express passenger trains on the Dijon-Nancy-Metz corridor. The remainder of their work is freight haulage on the same routes where they penetrate as far as Thionville and to certain yards on the German border. Unlike their sisters at Chalindrey depot, the BB 25150s, which work freight on the same corridor, they are not authorised, normally, to travel south of Dijon on the Sud-Est region. BB 25108 is seen here about to couple up to a train for the north at Dijon Ville station.

Class BB 25150

Number series: BB 25151-BB 25195 (45)
Built by: MTE
Introduced:
1967-69 25151-70
1974 25171-75
1976/77 25176-95
Type: Bo-Bo
Length:
25151-70 16.2m (53ft 2in)
25171-75 16.68m (54ft 9in)
25176-95 16.73m (54ft 10in)
Wheelbase: 12.4m (40ft 8in)
Wheel diameter: 1.25m (4ft 1in)
Weight in running order: 85-89 tonnes

UIC power rating:
Under 1,500V dc 3,400kW (4,560hp)
Under 25kV ac 4,130kW (5,540hp)
Maximum speed: 130km/h (81mph)
Pantograph types:
dc AM [illegible] single arm
ac AM18U single arm
Nominal supply voltages:
1,500V dc
25kV ac 50Hz
Depots of allocation: CH, CY
Works responsible: Hellemmes
Livery: Blue green with dark grey round cab windows and either with aluminium trim or lined in white. Now appearing in pale grey lined in orange as per BB 9280

Class BB 25150 was built as a development of the BB 25100s. The first batch, BB 25151-70, look identical but contain several internal changes including differences in the electrical system and gear ratio. There is no easy way to tell this first batch from BB 25100, and this complicates matters as most of the batch are allocated to Chalindrey depot and work freight on the Thionville-Metz-Dijon corridor. However, unlike BB 25100, this class is authorised to work south of Dijon and regularly reaches Sibelin and Chasse marshalling yards to the south of Lyon. Although the Chalindrey locomotives have no regular passenger workings, a number are drafted into action in the Alps during the winter sports season and work side by side with Chambéry allocated members of the same class. It is under these circumstances that BB 25151 is seen here on depot at St Gervais-le Fayet.

The second batch, Nos BB 25171-75, differ from the first in having reinforced buffer beams, like Class BB 16000, and large central grilles which protrude from the sides. All are allocated to Chambéry depot and together with their sister engines they work all locomotive hauled trains over the Alpine branches from Evian and St Gervais only as far as Lyon and Dijon, handing over to pure dc locomotives for long distance workings. BB 25172 is pictured here having just arrived at St Gervais with a train of couchettes from Lille.

The final development of the class saw the frontal aluminium trim being dropped in favour of white 'moustaches' and yellow numbers and SNCF lettering. A broad white band has also been added at headlight level. The overall effect can be judged from this photograph of No BB 25191 at St Gervais with a winter sports special train.

Class BB 25200

Number series: BB 25201-BB 25251 (51)
Built by: MTE
Introduced:
1965-67 25201-25246
1974 25247-25251
Type: Bo-Bo
Length:
25201-46 16.2m (53ft 2in)
25247-51 16.68m (54ft 9in)
Wheelbase: 12.4m (40ft 8in)
Wheel diameter: 1.25m (4ft 1in)
Weight in running order: 85-88 tonnes
UIC power rating:
Under 1,500V dc 3,400kW (4,560hp)
Under 25kV ac 4,130kW (5,540hp)

Maximum speed: 160km/h (99mph)
Pantograph type:
dc AM18B single arm
ac AM18U single arm
Nominal supply voltages:
1,500V dc
25kV ac 50Hz
Depot of allocation: MR
Works responsible: Hellemmes
Livery: Blue green with aluminium trim and dark grey round cab windows. Now appearing in pale grey lined in orange as per BB 9280

Class BB 25200 are similar to Classes BB 25100 and BB 25150 in both looks and inner workings but were built for a different operating area and therefore have different gear ratios and a higher speed. They are now all allocated to Montrouge depot and work express passenger trains on the Paris Montparnasse-Rennes/Nantes, and the Nantes-Tours routes, although the fastest trains out of Montparnasse are now hauled by Class BB 22200. This move has cascaded BB 25200 locomotives onto a greater number of freight workings than before, over the same routes but with continuation around Paris which takes them onto the other four regions and as far north as Amiens. They were built in two batches which are identical, externally, to the first two batches of Class BB 25150. Confusion is unlikely to occur at present as the two classes are only seen together in works. However in the near future some members of the class are to be modified for push-pull operation of Corail stock on the Lyon-Grenoble line, where they may be seen with Class BB 25150. Here No BB 25231 is caught on a relief holiday train at Rennes.

Class BB 25500

Number series: BB 25501-BB 25694 (194)
Built by: Alsthom
Introduced: 1964-1976
Type: B-B
Length:
25501-25544 14.7m (48ft 3in)
25545-25587 14.94m (49ft 0in)
25588-25694 15.57m (51ft 1in)
Wheelbase: 10.108m (33ft 2in)
Wheel diameter: 1.1m (3ft 7in)
Weight in running order: 79 tonnes
UIC power rating:
25501-25530 2,610kW (3,500hp)
25531-25694 2,940hp (3,950hp)
Maximum speed:
PV 90km/h (56mph)
GV 140km/h (87mph)
Pantograph types:
dc AM18B single arm
ac AM18U single arm
Nominal supply voltages:
1,500V dc
25kV ac 50Hz
Depots of allocation: LA, TS, AS, ME, MR, DN
Works responsible: Oullins
Livery: Blue/green lined in white with dark green panel round upper grilles and dark grey round cab windows. Now appearing in pale grey lined in orange as per class BB 17000

Dual-current Class BB 25500 was developed from Class BB 16500 after BB 16540 (now back to its original state) was converted to operate off both dc and ac. Experience gained from the experiment led the designers to make the body more resistant and to use silicon rectifiers instead of ignitrons The Class is mainly used on freight, particularly on trains which cross Paris from dc to ac or vice-versa. Marseille allocated locomotives are used on push-pull trains on the Côte D'Azur, Montrouge members on suburban trains out of Paris Montparnasse and Dijon locomotives on passenger and freight towards Besançon and Frasne. However, they are not usually used south of Tours on the Sud Ouest region or over the Est region except for short distance penetrations. There are three main batches within the class which correspond to the first two and last batches of Class BB 8500. They can be distinguished from Class BB 8500 by the lack of lightning conductor boxes forward of the pantographs. No BB 25504, at Lille (Fives) depot, in grey livery is one of the first batch, BB 25501- BB 25544, with small lateral grilles grouped in pairs.

The second batch, Nos BB 25545-BB 25587, is very similar to the first, but these locomotives have a reinforced buffer beam which projects slightly from the cab front. They also have yellow stickers instead of cast numbers and letters on the sides. This latter distinction is disappearing as locomotives of the first batch are also now receiving stickers. Locomotives will also lose their cast letters and figures as they are repainted in the new livery of pale grey lined in orange like that applied to Class BB 17000. The illustration shows No BB 25573, again at Lille, which is visited daily by members based at LA, TS and AS.

The final batch, Nos BB 25588-BB 25694, is easily identified by the longer cabs and the single, large lateral grille fitted to its members. BB 25663 of Achères depot is seen passing Juvisy yard in Paris with a block train for the Ouest region. Notice that it has both its dc (rear) and ac pantographs raised. This is normally done as a train starts, to spread the high current needed.

Class CC 40100

Number series: CC 40101-CC 40110 (10)
Former numbers: CC 27001-CC 27004 (40101-4)
Built by: Alsthom/Jeumont
Introduced:
1964 CC 40101-4
1969-70 CC 40105-10
Type: C-C
Length: 22.03m (72ft 3in)
Wheelbase: 17.556m (57ft 7in)
Wheel diameter: 1.1m (3ft 7in)
Weight in running order: 109 tonnes
UIC power rating:
40101-40104 3,710kW (4,985hp)
40105-40110 4,480kW (6,020hp)
Maximum speed: 160km/h (99mph)
Pantograph type:
dc AM18B single arm
ac AM18U single arm
Nominal supply voltages:
France 1,500V dc
25kV ac 50Hz
Belgium 3,000V dc
Germany 15kV ac 16Hz
Depot of allocation: LE
Works responsible: Hellemmes
Livery: Bare stainless steel with red grilles, side stripe and frontal panel. Yellow 'moustache' on front end

These impressive machines are amongst the most powerful and, at over 72ft, are certainly the longest locomotives on SNCF. Built to work off four different voltages for work into Belgium, Holland and Germany, they are now restricted to express passenger trains between Paris and Brussels or Liège, sharing this work with SNCB (Belgian National Railways) engines which work down to Paris. Although the two batches within the class have different power ratings and, indeed, gear ratios, there is no obvious way of telling them apart. Originally, the first four members had small cabside windows, but on passage through works these have been eliminated. Here the unmistakable lines of the class, in the form of CC 40107 *Bayonne*, are seen at Aulnoye in Northern France.

Class A1AA1A 62000

Number series: A1AA1A 62001-62100 (69)
Former numbers: 040DA 1-040DA 100
Built by: Baldwin (USA)
Introduced: 1946-47
Type: A1A-A1A
Length: [illegible]
Wheelbase: 13.336m (43ft 9in)
Wheel diameter: 1.1m (3ft 7in)
Weight in running order: 110 tonnes
UIC power rating: 380kW (510hp)
Engine: Baldwin 606 NA of 560kW (750hp)
Transmission: Electric
Maximum speed: 96km/h (60mph)
Depots of allocation: LB, TV, SG, LP
Works responsible: No longer overhauled
Livery: Dark green lined in yellow with yellow buffer beams

This class, known as 'Baldwins' were built by the Americans to help with reparations after World War 2 and, like most US designs, have been extremely hardy, being the oldest diesels operating on SNCF today. They can be easily recognised by their full height bonnets compared with the lower ones of the BB 63000 group, and by their distinctive engine noise which is not unlike a badly maintained BR Class 25! These locomotives are used for shunting in major stations and marshalling yards as well as a few short trip freights. Their home territory includes Le Bourget (Paris), Mulhouse, Strasbourg, Woippy (near Metz), Somain (south-east of Lille) and particularly, for British visitors, around Dunkerque where they unload the Sealink ferry (see introduction). Here, A1AA1A 62094 has been caught at Somain.

Class BB 63000

Number series: BB 63001-BB 63250 (250)
Former numbers: 040 DE 1-158 (63001-158)
Built by: Brissonneau and Lotz/Sulzer
Introduced: 1953-64
Type: Bo-Bo
Length: 14.68m (48ft 2in)
Wheelbase: 10.1m (33ft 2in)
Wheel diameter: 1.05m (3ft 5in)
Weight in running order: 64-69 tonnes
UIC power rating:
335kW (480hp) 63001-63108
435kW (585hp) 63109-63195
445kW (600hp) 63196-63250

Engine:
Sulzer 6LDA22B of 440kW (590hp) 63001-72
Sulzer 6LDA22C of 440kW (590hp) 63073-108
Sulzer 6LDA22C of 535kW (720hp) 63109-28
Sulzer 6LDA22D of 535kW (720hp) 63129-95
Sulzer 6LDA22E of 550kW (740hp) 63196-250
Transmission: Electric
Maximum speed: 80km/h (50mph)
Depots of allocation: VE, TS, NS, ME, PS, DN, CY, CH, LV, LS, LA
Works responsible: Sotteville
Livery: Dark green lined in yellow with yellow buffer beams.
Now appearing in orange with dark brown upper body lined in pale grey

The BB 63000 group of 853 locomotives, including BB 63400 & BB 63500, are SNCF's standard engines for 'manoeuvres' – shunting, empty stock and trip freight workings. As such, they can be found anywhere in France, at all the most important stations and marshalling yards, although in smaller numbers on the dc network where electric locomotives are often used. Whereas the main difference between BB 63000 and BB 63400 and 63500 is the former's less powerful Sulzer engine, there are few obvious visible differences between sub-series. The clearest are the thicker yellow band at the top of the bonnet and single exhaust pipe just in front of the cab windows, both of which are clear on the photograph below of No BB 63187 on station pilot duties at Lille. These multi-purpose locomotives have been successful and were exported to Spain, Portugal, Luxembourg and Yugoslavia as well as other, further-flung, countries.

Class BB 63400

Number series: BB 63401-BB 63423 (23)
Former numbers: 040DE 401-423
Built by: Brissonneau & Lotz
Introduced: 1959-60
Type: Bo-Bo
Length: 14.68m (48ft 2in)
Wheelbase: 10.1m (33ft 2in)
Wheel diameter: 1.05m (3ft 5in)
Weight in running order: 68 tonnes
UIC power rating: 450kW (605hp)
Engine: MGO V12SH of 605kW (810hp)
Transmission: Electric
Maximum speed: 80km/h (50mph)
Depots of allocation: NT, LI, BX, SF, RC
Works responsible: Nevers
Livery: Dark green lined in yellow with yellow buffer beams
Now appearing in orange with dark brown upper body lined in pale grey

Class BB 63400s is a variation on the '63000' group which came after BB 63500 started to be produced and, in fact, differ from that class in only very minor details which are not visible. They are distinguishable from Class BB 63000 by the narrower yellow stripe on the bonnet and by the double exhaust pipes on the side of the cab next to the longer bonnet. They are used on exactly the same sort of duties as BB 63000s but can only be found at work around five centres, all in the west and south-west of France. The photograph shows BB 63406 on Nantes depot.

Class BB 63500

Number series: BB 63501-BB 64080 (580)
Former numbers: 040DE 501-770 (63501-770)
Built by: Brissonneau & Lotz
Introduced: 1956-71
Type: Bo-Bo
Length: 14.68m (48ft 2in)
Wheelbase: 10.1m (33ft 2in)
Wheel diameter: 1.05m (3ft 5in)
Weight in running order: 64-68 tonnes
UIC power rating: 450kW (605hp)
Engine: MGO V12SH of 605kW (810hp)
Transmission: Electric
Maximum speed: 80km/h (50mph)
Depots of allocation: NT, RS, CN, BX, SE, AN, SG, LP, LI, MN, MZ, TE, LU, AS, NI, VX, LV
Works responsible: Nevers
Livery: Dark green lined in yellow with yellow buffer beams
Now appearing in orange with dark brown upper body lined in pale grey

Class BB 63500 is a development of the BB 63000s with a more powerful MGO engine. Most of the class are very similar externally to BB 63000 except for the previously mentioned yellow bonnet stripe and double exhaust pipes. There are a few detail differences within this class. For instance, the last 100 or so of the class have no SNCF roundel on their front ends. Secondly, BB 63721-50, BB 63811-85 and BB 63981-64020 are fitted for working in multiple. As can be seen from the photograph of BB 63722 below, these locomotives can be identified by the additional cables and pipes on their buffer beams.

Class CC 65000

Number series: CC 65001-CC 65020 (18)
Former numbers: 060-DB-1 to 060-DB-20
Built by: Alsthom/CAFL/SACM
Introduced: 1956-58
Type: Co-Co
Length: 19.814m (65ft 0in)
Wheelbase: 15.1m (49ft 6in)
Wheel diameter: 1.0[illegible] ([illegible]ft [illegible]in)
Weight in running order: 103 tonnes
UIC power rating: 970kW (1300hp)
Engines: 2x SACM MGO V12SR of 662kW (890hp) each
Transmission: Electric
Maximum speed:
PV 80km/h (50mph)
GV 130km/h ([illegible])
Depot of allocation: NT
Works responsible: No longer overhauled
Livery: Blue/grey lined in white and with white panel on front end. Dark grey at cab and roof level and in side and front panels. Red buffer beam.

Known as 'sous-marins' (submarines) to French railwaymen, perhaps because of their instantly recognisable bulbous-nosed outline, Class CC 65000 were some of the first medium-powered diesels to be built for SNCF. For many years now, their 'fief' has been the Nantes-La Rochelle-Bordeaux line and its branches but the class has been gradually losing work to more modern types and in 1985 only six were in regular service working freights, particularly around Saintes. However, it is expected that the stored members of the class, like those seen here on Nantes depot led by No CC 65009, will be soon revived for work on construction trains for the TGV-Atlantique line and associated electrification projects. This will probably mean them outstabling regularly at Le Mans and even in Paris where they have not been seen regularly for a long time.

Class CC 65500

Number series: CC 65501-CC 65535 (23)
Former numbers: 060DA 1 to 060DA 35, then CC 64001-CC 64035
Built by: CAFL/CEM/Sulzer
Introduced: 1955-59
Type: Co-Co
Length: 19.42m (63ft 8in)
Wheelbase: 14.188m (46ft 6in)
Wheel diameter: 1.2m (3ft 11in)
Weight in running order: 123 tonnes
UIC power rating: 1,188kW (1,595hp)
Engine: Sulzer 12LDA of 1,470kW (1,970hp)
Transmission: Electric
Maximum speed: 75km/h (47mph)
Depot of allocation: LP (see below)
Works responsible: No longer overhauled
Livery: Dark green lined in yellow with red buffer beam and SNCF symbol

This class was the first of SNCF's main-line diesels and was built specifically to haul freights on the 'Grande Ceinture' circular route avoiding the centre of Paris. As this route is now almost entirely electrified, they have lost this work and would now probably be withdrawn, given their age, if it were not for the TGV Sud Est scheme. During construction, they were drafted into service on engineering trains and about 10 have continued to work on the Sud-Est region since, working off Dijon or Chambéry depots although staying tied to their home depot of La Plaine. The remainder have remained working or stored at La Plaine, or hired out to coal mines in the Lorraine basin. It is now expected that at least a proportion of the class will have a continued lease of life working, like Class CC 65000, on construction trains for the TGV-Atlantique project. One point of interest in this class for British railfans is that they have a powerplant which was the precursor of the engine which powered BR Class 44, and which was further developed for Classes 45, 46 and 47. Nos CC 65506 and CC 65529 are seen together on Chambéry depot. Notice that both have the last two digits of their numbers painted prominently on their front ends, probably for the benefit of construction crews.

Class BB 66000

Number series: BB 66001-BB 66318 (307)
Former numbers: 040DG 1 to 040DG 37 (BB 66001-BB 66037)
Built by: CAFL/CEM/Alsthom/Fives-Lille-Cail/SACM
Introduced: 1960-68
Type: Bo-Bo
Length: 14.898m (48ft 10in)
Wheelbase: 11.06m (36ft 3in)
Wheel diameter: 1.1m (3ft 7in)
Weight in running order: 66/67 tonnes
UIC power rating: 830kW (1,115hp)
Engine: MGO V16BSHR of 1,030kW (1,380hp)
Transmission: Electric
Maximum speed: 120km/h (75mph)
Depots of allocation: TL, VX, AN, SG, NS, LU, SE, LI, LA, CH, NT
Works responsible: Nevers
Livery: Blue/grey with dark grey roof and solebar, white lining and frontal flash and red buffer beam

Class BB 66000 are light, mixed-traffic diesels which are equally at home on short passenger trains or, double-headed, on heavy freight. However, they are not fitted for electric train heating and so are becoming uncommon on passenger duties which will soon be confined to Class BB 66400. They can be seen in most of France, although certain depots only have Class BB 66400. It is difficult to tell Class BB 66000 from BB 66400 and BB 66600. If the photograph of No BB 66017 above is compared with that of BB 66411 on the opposite page, it is possible to see that BB 66017 has a different pattern of grilles along the bonnets, one door panel in the nose instead of two, a different cabside window design, no grilles on the cabside, no secondary bogie suspension and no ETH cable under the right-hand buffer. Unfortunately, these are not all sure guides for distinguishing a Class BB 66000. In the photograph below, it can be seen that several differences exist between BB 66149 (front) and BB 66115 (behind) seen here together at Sotteville.

Class BB 66400

Number series: BB 66401-BB 66506 (106)
Built by: CAFL/CEM/Alsthom/Fives-Lille-Cail/SACM
Introduced: 1968-71
Type: Bo-Bo
Length: 14.972m (49ft 1in)
Wheelbase: 11.06m (36ft 3in)
Wheel diameter: 1.1m (3ft 7in)
Weight in running order: 64 tonnes
UIC power rating: 830kW (1,115hp)
Engine: MGO V16BSHR of 1,030kW (1,380hp)
Transmission: Three-phase electric
Maximum speed: 120km/h (75mph)
Depots of allocation: LS, CH, LP, NT, SE, NS, TE
Works responsible: Nevers
Livery: Blue/grey with dark grey roof and solebar, white lining and frontal flash and red buffer beam

After a small number of BB 66000s served as prototypes, it was decided to adopt certain modifications for the future Class BB 66400. These included three-phase electric transmission and secondary rubber suspension similar to that on Class BB 67400. Most, but not all, are also fitted with electric train heating and for working push-pull trains. Duties are similar to those of BB 66000 but there is more work on passenger trains, particularly on push-pull workings in the north-west of France and on suburban services out of Paris Est. These trains are rarely very long as providing heat and light deprives a locomotive of one third of its power! Although the suspension and ETH cable are clearly seen on this photograph of No BB 66411 at Lille (La Délivrance), it is not easy to tell this class from later members of Class BB 66000 at a distance.

Class BB 66600

Number series: BB 66604-BB 66616 (11)
Former numbers: Converted from BB 66000 locomotives at random
Built by: CAFL/CEM/SEMT/Alsthom/Fives-Lille-Cail
Introduced: 1960-62
Type: Bo-Bo
Length: 14.[illegible]m (48ft 10in)
Wheelbase: 11.06m (36ft 3in)
Wheel diameter: 1.1m (3ft 7in)
Weight in running order: 71 tonnes
UIC power rating: 890kW (1,195hp)
Engine: SEMT 12PA4 of 1,100kW (1,480hp)
Transmission: Electric
Maximum speed: 120km/h (75[illegible])
Depot of allocation: [illegible]
Works responsible: Nevers
Livery: Blue/grey with dark grey roof and solebar, white lining and frontal flash and red buffer beams

Class BB 66600 is a small group of locomotives converted from BB 66000s in order to try out a different, slightly more powerful, engine. This experiment has not been followed through, and it seems that the class will be up for moderately early withdrawal. Because of their origins, these locomotives are externally identical to BB 66000s but if heard in action, can be distinguished by their much more rattly engine sound. Another feature, which is difficult for the casual observer to detect, is that the class has four driving positions in the cab against two for Classes BB 66000 & BB 66400. Their diagram from Nîmes depot covers only freight, most of which is on the line towards Alès and Clermont Ferrand. Here No BB 66614 hauls a freight through Nîmes station.

Class BB 66700

Number series: BB 66701-BB 66740 (5)
Former numbers: Converted from BB 66000 locomotives at random
Built by: CAFL/CEM/Sulzer/Alsthom/ Fives-Lille-Cail/SACM
Introduced: 1985 – being delivered
Type: Bo-Bo
Length: 14.898m (48ft 10in)
Wheelbase: 11.06m (36ft 3in)
Wheel diameter: 1.1m (3ft 7in)
Weight in running order: 71 tonnes
UIC power rating: 830kW (1,115hp)
Engine: MGO V16BSHR of 1,030kW (1,380hp)
Transmission: Electric
Maximum speed: 90km/h (56mph)
Depot of allocation: VX
Works responsible: Nevers
Livery: Orange with dark brown roof and pale grey lining and solebar

Locomotives of Class BB 66700, at present being introduced, have been converted from Class BB 66000 for shunting duties in SNCF's marshalling yards as BB 63000s have been found to lack the power to move around the heaviest freight trains. The conversion involves reduction of the gear ratio thus lowering the maximum speed, modification of cab controls and the installation of remote control gear. More obvious to the observer is the removal of cast number plates and SNCF symbol and the new orange-yellow livery which easily distinguishes this class from other locomotives in the BB 66000 group. The photograph shows No BB 66701, newly ex-works, in the company of a BB 66000, at Dijon depot.

Class BB 67000

Number series: BB 67001-BB 67097 (72)
Built by: Brissoneau & Lotz/MTE/SEMT
Introduced: 1963-68
Type: B-B
Length: 17.09m (56ft 1in)
Wheelbase: 12.2m (40ft 0in)
Wheel diameter: 1.15m ([illegible]ft [illegible]in)
Weight in running order: [illegible]0 tonnes
UIC power rating: 1,240kW (1,665hp)
Engine: SEMT 16PA4 of 1,470kW (1,975hp)
Transmission: Electric
Maximum speed: 90km/h (56mph)
Depots of allocation: NS, ME, RS
Works responsible: Nevers
Livery: Blue/grey with dark grey lateral grilles and round cab windows and white lateral lines and frontal flashes

The standard diesel workhorse of the SNCF, locomotives of the BB 67000/67200/67300/67400 group are as ubiquitous in France as are Class 47s in Britain. Differences between sub-series appeared gradually as they were built over a period of 12 years. The first series, BB 67000, originally ran from 67001-67124, but the class is now reduced to 72 examples mainly due to conversions to Classes BB 67200 and BB 67300. Although built with two speed ranges, like Class BB 67300, for mixed traffic duties, BB 67000 locomotives are now fixed on the lower speed/higher tractive effort régime and are restricted to freight duties. Rennes examples can be seen throughout most of Brittany, often working in pairs, whilst Nevers and Marseille locomotives work much of the freight traffic in the Massif Central and on diesel lines in the Rhone area. The photograph shows Nevers locomotive BB 67017 at Villeneuve St Georges in the Paris suburbs. Although very similar to the other '67' groups of locomotives, BB 67000s can be distinguished by the small 'T' shapes in the body above the the bogie centres.

Class BB 67200

Number series: BB 67201-BB 67230 (30)
Former numbers: Converted from Class BB 67000 at random
Built by: Brissoneau & Lotz/MTE/SEMT
Introduced: 1980-84
Type: B-B
Length: 17.09m (56ft 1in)
Wheelbase: 12.2m (40ft 0in)
Wheel diameter: 1.15m (3ft 9in)
Weight in running order: 80 tonnes
UIC power rating: 1,240kW (1,665hp)
Engine: SEMT 16PA4 of 1,470kW (1,975hp)
Transmission: Electric
Maximum speed: 90km/h (56mph)
Depot of allocation: NS
Works responsible: Nevers
Livery: Blue/grey with dark grey lateral grilles and round cab windows, and white lateral lines and frontal flashes

The 30 members of Class BB 67200 were converted from BB 67000s and are specially equipped with cab signalling and radio for work on the 'Ligne à Grande Vitesse' from the Paris suburbs to Lyon. They are used on permanent way maintenance trains on the line at night and on other freight duties during the daytime. They are usually seen close to the TGV line at locations such as Villeneuve, Laroche-Migennes, Dijon, Mâcon and Lyon but can also be spotted, occasionally, in much further-flung places where Nevers-based BB 67000 locomotives also work. They can be identified by their deep, solid buffer beams and transfer numbers and letters on their sides where other members of the '67' group have cast figures. All members of this class are fitted with small snowploughs. In addition, at the end of the locomotive with two white stripes an aerial is fitted to the roof just above the central headlight and there exists a group of three jumper cable connections, similar to that on the front of CC 21002, on the right-hand side of the cab front. Unfortunately, this is not visible on this photograph of No BB 67206 on Vénissieux depot.

Class BB 67300

Number series: BB 67301-BB 67390 (90)
Former numbers: 67371-90 were converted at random from Class BB 67000
Built by: Brissoneau & Lotz/MTE/SEMT
Introduced: 1967-79
Type: B-B
Length: 17.09m (56ft [illegible])
Wheelbase: 12.2m (40ft 0in)
Wheel diameter: 1.15m (3ft 9in)
Weight in running order: 80 tonnes
UIC power rating: 1,440kW (1,935hp)
Engine: SEMT 16PA4 of 1,765kW (2,370hp)
Transmission: Three-phase electric
Maximum speed:
PV 90km/h (56mph)
GV 140km/h (87mph)
Depots of allocation: CY, NT, TS, CN
Works responsible: Nevers
Livery: Blue/grey with dark grey lateral grilles and round cab windows, and white lateral lines and frontal flashes

Class BB 67300 was the first modification of the '67' series and mainly differs from BB 67000 in being fitted with an alternator for electric train heating as well as having an uprated version of the 16PA4 engine, three-phase transmission and a higher maximum speed. After a prototype was converted from a BB 67000, 70 Class BB 67300s were built new, then another twenty were converted from BB 67000 locomotives. Only two small marks of identification distinguish them from Class BB 67000 – the lack of the 'T' shape in the body above the bogies and the ETH cable fitted next to the right hand buffer. This class can be found equally on freight and passenger duties throughout Normandy, on the Caen-Le Mans-Tours-Nevers transversal, on the Nantes-La Rochelle-Bordeaux line and branches, and on diesel lines in the southern Alps, particularly those to Bourg St Maurice and Briançon.

Below one of the converted members of the class, No BB 67386, stands in Nantes at the head of a train from Toulouse to Rennes.

Class BB 67400

Number series: BB 67401-BB 67632 (230)
Built by: Brissoneau & Lotz/MTE/SEMT
Introduced: 1969-75
Type: B-B
Length: 17.09m (56ft 1in)
Wheelbase: 12.3m (40ft 4in)
Wheel diameter: 1.26m (4ft 2in)
Weight in running order: 83 tonnes
UIC power rating: 1,525kW (2,050hp)
Engine: SEMT 16PA4 of 1,765kW (2,370hp)
Transmission: Three-phase electric
Maximum speed: 140km/h (87mph)
Depots of allocation: VX, BX, CN, NS, RS, CH, LU, ME, NI, LI, SG
Works responsible: Sotteville
Livery: Blue/grey with dark grey round cab windows and lateral grilles, and white lateral stripes and frontal flashes

Class BB 67400 was the final development of the BB 67000 series and members of the class were the last new diesels to be built for SNCF. They are very similar to the previous locomotives, the most obvious visual difference being the improved secondary suspension. The difference between the bogies on No BB 67385 and on BB 67553 can be clearly seen in the photograph below.

Other changes include slightly greater length, single gear ratio and forced air ventilation of traction motors. Another identification mark is the higher number and letter position on the sides as seen on BB 67619 at Lille (La Délivrance) depot. This class can be seen on freight and passenger work over much of France and couple in multiple with Class BB 67300. They will be particularly familiar to visitors to Calais and Boulogne where Longueau members are in charge of all express passenger trains.

Class A1AA1A 68000

Number series: A1AA1A 68001-A1AA1A 68085 (83)
Former numbers: 68082-85 were converted from A1AA1A 68500 at random
Built by: CAFL/CEM/Sulzer/Fives-Lille-Cail
Introduced: 1963-68
Type: A1A-A1A
Length: 17.92m (58ft 9in)
Wheelbase: 12.5m (41ft 0in)
Driving wheel diameter: 1.25m (4ft 1in)
Centre wheel diameter: 0.95m (3ft 1in)
Weight in running order: 104 tonnes
UIC power rating: 1,660kW (2,230hp)
Engine: Sulzer 12LVA24 of 1,950kW (2,620hp)
Transmission: Electric
Maximum speed: 130km/h (81mph)
Depots of allocation: NT, LP, CH, TS
Works responsible: Sotteville
Livery: Blue/grey with dark grey lateral grilles and round cab windows and white lateral stripes and frontal flashes

Class A1AA1A 68000 were, with Class A1AA1A 68500, originally SNCFs most powerful diesel passenger locomotives, but with the passage of time they have been replaced either by Class CC 72000 or by electric traction where lines have been electrified. Nowadays they have had their steam heating equipment removed without receiving electric heating gear, so are restricted to freight traffic. They are especially used on the transversal Caen-Le Mans-Tours-Nevers route, on the Paris-Troyes-Belfort line, in northern Paris and in southern Brittanny. At Chalindrey depot they are used in multiple with Class 68500 on a common diagram. Externally, they are very similar to the BB 67000 group but can be identified by the secondary suspension over the middle of their bogies and their deeper, more solid buffer beams, both of which are very clear on A1AA1A 68009 seen here at Nantes depot. They are, however, identical externally to Class 68500. Indeed, a few 68500s have recently been converted to 68000s by the simple method of changing a Sulzer engine for the original AGO unit. This may be done again in the future if the results are found to be satisfactory.

Class A1AA1A 68500

Number series: A1AA1A 68502-A1AA1A 68528 (24)
Built by: CAFL/CEM/SACM/Fives-Lille-Cail
Introduced: 1964-68
Type: A1A-A1A
Length: 17.92m (58ft 9in)
Wheelbase: 12.5m (41ft 0in)
Driving wheel diameter: 1.25m (4ft 1in)
Centre wheel diameter: 0.95m (3ft 1in)
Weight in running order: 102 tonnes
UIC power rating: 1,645kW (2,210hp)
Engine: AGO 12DSHR of 1,985kW (2,670hp)
Transmission: Electric
Maximum speed: 130km/h (81mph)
Depot of allocation: CH
Works responsible: Sotteville
Livery: Blue/grey with dark grey lateral grilles and round cab windows and white lateral stripes and frontal flashes

As noted previously, this class is identical to the A1AA1A 68000s in all but its AGO engine. The whole class is allocated to Chalindrey and together with the 13 members of Class 68000 at that depot work freight on the Paris-Troyes-Belfort main line, as well as on the Belfcrt-Blainville (near Nancy), Troyes-Chalons-sur-Marne and Chalindrey-St Dizier lines. They are particularly used for hauling heavy trains of bottled mineral water from the source towns of Vittel and Contrexéville. No A1AA1A 68504, which is pictured here at Noisy-le-Sec near Paris, is one of five fitted with mini snowploughs for work in the Vosges mountains around Epinal in winter.

Class BB 71000

Number series: BB 71001-BB 71030 (15)
Built by: Fives-Lille-Cail/CFD
Introduced: 1965-66
Type: B-B
Length: 11.85m (38ft 10in)
Wheelbase: 7.6m (24ft 11in)
Wheel diameter: 0.86m (2ft 10in)
Weight in running order: 66 tonnes
UIC power rating: 400kW (540hp)
Engine: Poyaud V12 of 615kW (830hp)
Transmission: Mechanical
Maximum speed: 80km/h (50mph)
Depot of allocation: NS
Works responsible: No longer overhauled
Livery: Dark green lined in yellow with yellow buffer beam and red SNCF roundel

This unusual design, somewhere between a shunter and a low powered freight locomotive, has not been a conspicuous success with SNCF. The class is being withdrawn after locomotives have been in service less than 20 years and have travelled only 300,000 miles. The class has always been consigned to obscure trip freight duties on little known secondary lines and all members are likely to disappear without fuss by 1988. At present, the remaining units are concentrated in two centres, Vichy and Autun. The illustration shows BB 71028 on TS depot before the class disappeared from there in 1985.

Class CC 72000

Number series: CC 72001-CC 72092 (91)
Built by:
Alsthom/SACM except
Alsthom/SEMT (72075)
Introduced: 1967-74
Type: C-C
Length: 20.19m (66ft 3in)
Wheelbase: 15.206m (49ft 11in)
Wheel diameter: 1.14m (3ft 9in)
Weight in running order: 114 tonnes except 72075 118 tonnes
UIC power rating: 2,250kW (3,020hp) except 72075 3,100kW (4,160hp)
Engine: AGO V16ESHR of 2,650kW (3,560hp) except 72075: Pielstick 12PA6280 of 3,530kW (4,740hp)
Transmission: Electric
Maximum speed:
72001-20 140km/h (87mph)
72021-92 160km/h (99mph)
Depots of allocation: VX, CH, RS
Works responsible: Sotteville
Livery: Blue/grey with dark grey roof and side panel lined in white and with white lateral and nose stripe

Class CC 72000 are SNCF's most powerful diesels and are easily distinguished from other diesels by their modern outline, similar to recent French electric classes. Designed for passenger services on the most important non-electrified lines such as Lyon-Nantes, Lyon-Bordeaux, Paris-Belfort-Basle, Rennes-Brest and Nantes-Quimper, they are also used to haul heavy freight on the same routes and their branches. Although all outwardly identical, two variants to the standard design exist. The first 20 locomotives of the class are restricted to 140km/h and are mainly based at Vénissieux (Lyon). More interestingly, No CC 72075 is fitted, experimentally, with an engine of 4,740hp which makes it the world's most powerful single power unit in a diesel locomotive. CC 72075 is allocated to Rennes depot where drivers have nicknamed it the 'Boeing'. It does a return journey to Brest every day and must be replaced by two Class BB 67400s if it is ever indisposed.

No CC 72028 is seen being detached from a Brest-Paris train at Rennes.

Class Y 2200

Number series: Y 2201-Y 2340 (52)
Built by:
Moyse/Poyaud (2201-2249)
Decauville/Poyaud (2250-2320)
Decauville/Alsthom (2321-2340)
Introduced: 1956-60
Type: B (0-4-0)
Length: 5.78m (18ft 11in)
Wheelbase: 3m (9ft 10in)
Wheel diameter: 1.05m (3ft 5in)
Weight in running order: 16 tonnes
UIC power rating: 38kW (50hp)

Engine:
Poyaud 2PDT of 44kW (60hp) Y 2201-2320
Agrom of 40kW (55hp) Y 2321-2340
Transmission: Mechanical
Maximum speed: 50km/h (31mph)
Depots of allocation: LV, CH, MZ, SG, LP, AS, LM, SE, CN, BX, TE, TB, DN, NS, VX, CY, ME, AN, NI
Works responsible: No longer overhauled
Livery: Dark green lined in yellow with yellow buffer beams

These shunters are the smallest standard gauge locomotives in use on SNCF metals and can be recognised firstly by their diminutive size. In fact, few are likely to be seen by the casual traveller as they are used mainly for light duties within depot and workshop areas, and because they are slowly being withdrawn. The photograph shows two examples, Nos Y 2274 and Y 2300, on Rennes depot. The reader can see both short and long bonnets in the picture. Although both these engines have yellow lining, a small number of the class are painted in plain dark green.

Class Y 2400

Number series: Y 2401-Y 2519 (112)
Built by: Decauville/Alsthom
Introduced: 1962-69
Type: B (0-4-0)
Length: 7.18m (23ft 7in)
Wheelbase: 3m (9ft 10in)
Wheel diameter: 1.05m (3ft 5in)
Weight in running order: 17 tonnes
UIC power rating: 40kW (55hp)
Engine: Agrom of 45kW (60hp)
Transmission: Mechanical
Maximum speed: 50km/h (31mph)
Depots of allocation: CH, SG, LP, LU, AS, SE, RS, PS, TS, BX, LI, TE, TB, VE, DN, NS, VX, CY, ME, AN, NI
Works responsible: Nevers
Livery: Dark green lined in yellow with yellow buffer beams

This class can be distinguished from Y 2200 by several features, but particularly by their longer bonnet. The greater difficulty is in differentiating between Classes Y 2400 and Y 5100 which are very similar. The principal differences are in the front of the long bonnet where Class Y 2400 has a small square projection whereas Y 5100 has a grille flush with the front, in the number of lateral grilles of which Y 5100 has more, in the exhaust funnel in front of the cab which is shorter and narrower on Y 2400 and, less obviously, in the yellow lining which runs along the full height of the cab edge on Y 5100 but stops at bonnet height on Y 2400. Like Class Y 2200, these locomotives are used for rather light shunting duties, often out of the public gaze. Here, No Y 2456 is seen on Villeneuve depot, clearly out of use, and back to back with a Y 2200.

Class Y 5100 & Y 5200

Number series:
Y 5101-Y 5162 (62)
Y 5201-Y 5216 (16)
Built by: De Dietrich/Poyaud
Introduced: 1960-63
Type: B (0-4-0)
Length: 7,18m (23ft 7in)
Wheelbase: [illegible]
Wheel diameter: 1.05m (3ft 5in)
Weight in running order: 20 tonnes
UIC power rating: 59kW (80hp)
Engine: Poyaud 4PYT of 81kW (110hp)
Transmission: Hydraulic
Maximum speed: 18km/h (11mph)
Depots of allocation: LV, CH MN, MZ, TV, SG, LP, LS, LU, AS, LM, SE, CN, RS, LR, NT, PS, [illegible], NI
Works responsible: Nevers
Livery: Dark green lined in yellow with yellow buffer beams

As noted on the previous page, Classes Y 5100/Y 5200 are very similar to Y 2400, despite the obvious differences in power rating and transmission. The two batches Y 5101-62 and Y 5201-16 are identical despite being numerically separate. Again, like Y 2200 and Y 2400, the duties of this class restrict its members to work in depots and workshops. Here No Y 5214 is pictured on La Plaine depot.

Y 5143, which is allocated to La Villette depot, carries plates for the town of Millau on its cab sides. Although the plates are well finished, they are not in the official SNCF style and are therefore probably unofficial. It is certainly difficult to explain why a lowly shunter in the east of Paris should be named after a town 430 miles away in the Massif Central!

Class Y 6200, Y 6300 & Y 6400

Number series: Y 6201-Y 6297 (39)
Y 6301-Y 6330 (21)
Y 6401-Y 6627 (209)
Built by:
Billard (6201-59/6301-30)
Moyse (6261-6297)
De Dietrich (6401-30/6501-25)
Decauville (6431-6500)
SNCF (6626/6627)
Introduced: 1949-58
Type: B (0-4-0)
Length: 8.9m (29ft 2in)
Wheelbase: 3.54m (11ft 7in)
Wheel diameter: 1.05m (3ft 5in)
UIC power rating: 95kW (130hp)
Engine: Poyaud 6PDT of 132kW (180hp)
Transmission: Electric
Maximum speed: 60km/h (37mph)
Depots of allocation: LV, CH, MN, MZ, SG, LP, LS, LU, AS, LM, SE, CN, RS, LR, NT, PS, LA, TS, BX, LI, TE, TB, VE, DN, NS, VX, CY, ME, AN, NI
Works responsible: No longer overhauled
Livery: Dark green lined in yellow with yellow buffer beam

These medium-sized shunters, with a cab placed slightly off-centre, are now reaching the ripe old age of 35 and so are being retired in favour of Class Y 8000. Although split into three classes, locomotives are identical except for one detail – locomotives Y 6201-Y 6259 have cab side windows in three pieces, while the rest, like No Y 6614 in the illustration, have windows in two pieces. Opposite ends of these engines are quite different, the shorter bonnet being higher and without a grille. These shunters can be found almost anywhere on the SNCF network, as the list of depots indicates! Their duties include all but the heaviest shunting tasks in both freight and passenger stations.

Class Y 7100

Number series: Y 7101-Y 7310 (209)
Built by:
Billard (7101-7230)
Decauville (7231-7310)
Introduced: 1958-62
Type: B (0-4-0)
Length: 8.94m (29ft 4in)
Wheelbase: [illegible]
Wheel diameter: 1.05m (3ft 5in)
Weight in running order: 32 tonnes
UIC power rating: 129kW (175hp)
Engine: Poyaud 6PYT of 150kW (200hp)
Transmission: Hydromechanical
Maximum speed: 54km/h (34mph)
Depots of allocation: MN, MZ, LP, LS, LU, AS, SE, CN, PS, TS, BX, LI, TB, VE, DN, NS, VX, CY, ME, AN, NI
Works responsible: Nevers
Livery: Dark green lined in yellow with yellow buffer beams.
Now appearing in orange with dark brown upper body lined in pale grey

This class together with Class Y 7400, which is identical except for its different transmission, form the largest group of shunters at present in service in France. As such, they can be seen just about anywhere on the SNCF network on all sorts of shunting duties. These engines, like Class Y 8000, have one long bonnet and a short one on the other side of the cab. Although most of the class, like No Y 7125 seen below on La Plaine depot, are still in green livery, locomotives are slowly appearing in the attractive orange-yellow livery seen opposite on No Y 7601.

Classes Y 7001 & Y 7400

Number series:
Y 7001 (1)
Y 7401-Y 7888 (488)
Former number: Y 7001 was converted from Y 7192
Built by:
Billard (Y 7001)
Decauville (Y 7401-Y 7520)
De Dietrich (Y 7521-Y 7625)
Moyse (Y 7626-Y 7888)
Introduced:
1959 (Y 7001)
1963-72 (rest)
Type: B (0-4-0)
Length: 8.94m (29ft 4in)
Wheelbase: 3.685m (12ft 1in)
Wheel diameter: 1.05m (3ft 5in)
Weight in running order: 32 tonnes
UIC power rating: 129kW (175hp)
Engine: Poyaud 6PYT of 150kW (200hp)
Transmission: Mechanical
Maximum speed: 60km/h (37mph)
Depots of allocation: LV, CH, SG, LP, LS, LU, AS, LM, SE, RS, LR, NT, PS, LA, TS, BX, LI, TE, TB, VE, DN, NS, VX, CY, ME, AN, NI
Works responsible: Nevers
Livery: Dark green lined in yellow with yellow buffer beams.
Now appearing in orange with dark brown upper body lined in pale grey

After No Y 7192 was converted to be prototype Y 7001, SNCF decided to adopt the simpler mechanical transmission for Class Y 7400. Except for this, they remained identical to Class Y 7100. The photograph shows the 'short' end of No Y 7601 which was one of the first of the class to be repainted in orange, brown and grey livery.

Class Y 8000

Number series: Y 8001-Y 8285 (270)
Built by: Moyse or Fauvet Girel
Introduced: 1977 – being delivered
Type: B (0-4-0)
Length: 10.14m (33ft 3in)
Wheelbase: 5.54m (18ft 0in)
Wheel diameter: 1.05m (3ft 5in)
Weight in running order: 35 tonnes
UIC power rating: 161kW (215hp)

Engine: Poyaud V12520NS of 219kW (295hp)
Transmission: Hydraulic
Maximum speed:
PV 30km/h (19mph)
GV 60km/h (37mph)
Depots of allocation: MZ, LP, LU, SE, RS, TS, BX, DN, VX, ME, NI
Works responsible: Nevers
Livery: Orange with dark [illegible] body lined in pale grey

Class Y 8000 are the only new diesel locomotives being delivered to SNCF at present and are being built to replace older, less powerful shunters. Their power rating is at the top of the range for SNCF shunters, anything more powerful being classed as a 'locomoteur' (something between a shunter and locomotive) or locomotive. This high power, plus the ability to operate at up to 60km/h makes them suitable for light trip freights as well as heavy shunting duties. The reason for the change in constructor is that Moyse went bankrupt, leaving Fauvet-Girel, before this a sub-contractor, to pick up the pieces.

Although superficially similar to other recent classes of shunter (compare with the photograph of Y 7601), Y 8000s are significantly longer than previous classes and have lower bonnets which allow larger cab windows, giving better visibility. The greater length gives room for platforms at both ends to accommodate staff assisting in shunting movements. On Classes Y 7100/Y 7400, a platform only exists at the 'long' end. Two other features which distinguish Class Y 8000 are the large overhang of the cab roof and the panels above the buffer beams incorporating headlights, taillights and the locomotive number. The photograph on this page shows No Y 8056 at its home depot of Sotteville.

Class BA 11/12

Number series: BA 11-BA 12 (2)
Built by: Chemins de Fer Départmentaux
Introduced: 1952
Type: C (0-6-0)
Length: 6.0m (19ft 8in)
Wheelbase: 2.4m (7ft 10in)
Wheel diameter: 0.84m (2ft 9in)
Weight in running order: 17 tonnes
UIC power rating: 106kW (140hp)
Engine: Willème 517-F8 of 132kW (175hp)
Transmission: Mechanical
Maximum speed: 30km/h (19mph)
Depot of allocation: RN
Works responsible: Romorantin depot
Livery: Dark green lined in yellow with yellow buffer beams.

Although clearly numbered BA 11 and BA 12, these strange machines are officially numbered T 11/12 according to SNCF stock lists. The reason for this is not apparent to the author; there is a much better reason for them to have the BA prefix. These are metre gauge locomotives which work the line in central France known as the 'Le Blanc-Argent' after its original termini. Nowadays, the line runs from Salbris (on the Orléans-Vierzon line) to Buzançais, the section from Luçay-Le-Mâle to Buzançais only being open to freight traffic. The line is certainly a curiosity in the days of TGVs, but passenger traffic has increased regularly on the line in recent years which has led to the modernisation of the passenger railcars (Classes X 200-X 240). However, freight has declined considerably over the same period and it seems that a crunch decision will have to be taken soon over whether to renew or withdraw completely. In the meantime, interested parties can see 85-year old freight stock being hauled by the curious beasts of this and the following class. The photograph shows BA 12 arriving at Romorantin with a freight.

Class BA 13/14

Number series: BA 13/BA 14 (2)
Built by: Le Blanc-Argent (Romorantin)
Introduced: 1953
Type: C (0-6-0)
Length: 8.45m (27ft 9in)
Wheelbase: 3.48m (11ft 5in)
Wheel diameter: 0.94m (3ft 1in)
Weight in running order: 18 tonnes
UIC power rating: 106kW (140hp)
Engine: Willème 517-F8 of 132kW (175hp)
Transmission: Mechanical
Maximum speed: 30km/h (19mph)
Depot of allocation: RN
Works responsible: Romorantin depot
Livery: Dark green lined in yellow with yellow buffer beams

These two locomotives are even more curious than BA 11/12, having been built by the metre gauge line's own workshops on the chassis of withdrawn steam engines! They are used in common with BA 11/12 on freight trains between Buzançais and Romorantin, where goods are transhipped (mainly by hand!) between metre and standard gauge wagons. Although probably a large financial burden on SNCF and local authorities, this line is useful for testing metre gauge stock built in France for export. The illustrations show BA 13 in a rather desolate state on Romorantin depot.

Class X 200

Car type: XBD
Number: X 205
Length: 19.12m (62ft 9in)
Weight: 18 tonnes
Seating: 51 second
Usual formation: Single unit plus one trailer if necessary
Built by: De Dion/Willème

Introduced: 1947
UIC power rating: 106kW (140hp)
Engine: Willème 517F8 of 132kW (175hp)
Transmission: Mechanical
Maximum speed: 70km/h (43mph)
Depot of allocation: RN
Works responsible: Romorantin depot
Livery: Red below window level and cream above

For passenger services on its metre gauge line from Salbris to Luçay-le-Mâle (see Class BA 11/12), SNCF has a fleet of eight railcars of four different types. The oldest of these is X 205 which is the last of a class of four De Dion DC 2 single units which were sold to the line when the metre gauge Réseau Breton (a network based on the town of Carhaix) closed. Due to the introduction of Class X 240 and the refurbishment of Class X 210, X 205 is now only held in reserve for enthusiasts specials or for the replacement of one of the other units in the case of an exceptional breakdown. It is, therefore, usually to be found on depot at Romorantin, as it was here, in the photograph, together with other members of the class being cannibalised for spare parts. This unit is easily identified by its sloping front ends and by its red and cream livery which is now only shared with No X 224.

Classes X 210 & X 220

Car type:	XBD	XBD
Number series:	X 211-X 214 (4)	X 224
Weight:	21 tonnes	18 tonnes
Seating:	54 second	53 second
UIC power rating:	150kW (200hp)	82kW (110hp)
Engine:	Poyaud 6L520S1 of 185kW (250hp)	Willème 517F6 of 103kw (140hp)
Transmission:	Hydromechanical	Mechanical
Maximum speed:	85km/h ([illegible])	80km/h (50mph)
Livery:	Cream with chocolate brown panels on front end, round side windows and along solebar	Red below window level and cream above
Length:	18.535m (60ft 10in)	
Usual formation:	Single unit plus one trailer if necessary	
Built by:	Verney	
Introduced:	1950-51	
Depot of allocation:	RN	
Works responsible:	Romorantin	

These two classes represent the refurbished (X 210) and unrefurbished (X 220) versions of the same railcars. The refurbishment of X 211-214 took place in 1983/84 and included a new engine, transmission and interior as well as a new front end design and colour scheme. X 224 will remain unmodernised and has three front cab windows and headlights in a lower position as well as other less obvious differences, and, of course, its original red and cream livery. Class X 210 provide the normal passenger service on the line, together with Class X 240 with which they may work in multiple. Here X 211 stands in Salbris station with a train for Luçay-le-Mâle. No X 224, like X 205, remains in reserve and only operates if Class X 210 and X 240 railcars are unavailable for service.

Class X 240

Car type: XBD
Number series: X 241/X 242 (2)
Length: 18.27m (59ft 11in)
Weight: 25 tonnes
Seating: 52 second
Usual formation: Single unit plus one trailer if necessary
Built by: Socofer/CFD
Introduced: 1983-84
UIC power rating: 175kW (235hp)
Engine: Poyaud 6L520CS2
Transmission: Hydraulic
Maximum speed: 85km/h (53mph)
Depot of allocation: RN
Works responsible: Romorantin depot
Livery: Cream with chocolate brown panels on front end, round side windows and along solebar

These units were built for the modernisation of the passenger service on the line from Salbris to Luçay-le-Mâle, the plan also encompassing the modernisation of Class X 210. The design of Class X 240 is drawn from recent railcars built for Corsican Railways (CFC) but incorporates as many standard SNCF components as possible. For instance, the folding doors are taken from Corail coaches and the seats are identical to those in Class Z 6400 units. Their modern outline and, particularly, their greater height distinguish them readily from other railcars on the line. They share the main workings on the line with Class X 210. Here No X 241 is seen stabled in Salbris station.

Classes X 2100 & X 92100

Car type: XABD
Number series:
X 2101-X 2150 (49)
X 92101-X 92104 (4)
Length: 22.4m (73ft 6in)
Weight: 44 tonnes
Seating: 8 first; 48 second
Usual formation: Single unit plus up to three trailers
Built by: ANF/Saurer/Schneider
Introduced: 1980-83

UIC power rating: 330kW (445hp)
Engine: Saurer S1DHR of 440kW (590hp)
Transmission: Hydraulic
Maximum speed: 140km/h (87mph)
Depots of allocation: TE, LY, NT, RS
Works responsible: Bordeaux
Livery: Mid blue with white window band and pale grey panels between cab and side windows (see below for X 92101-2)

It may seem strange to readers that SNCF should want to continue the practice of running single units, like Class X 2100, towing trailers and therefore making run-round facilities necessary at all sorts of small country destinations. However, although the number of such workings will reduce with the replacement of Class X 3800, mainly by cascaded two-car sets, SNCF seems happy to order new single units. Class X 2100 has only been recently delivered and will be followed by an improved version, X 2200, as this book appears. X 2100 units can be found at work on stopping trains throughout Brittany's dieselised enclave, on the lines to the west of Lyon and around Toulouse, often with trailer cars and sometimes with Class X 2800 units, with which they are couplable. They are easily identifiable by their clean, modern lines and the irregular front end window pattern. Class X 2200 will be very similar but will appear in a completely different livery like that of the refurbished RGPs (Classes X 2720 & X 2770). The photograph shows X 2134 stabled at Rennes.

It is now common practice in France for regional councils and other 'third parties' to buy their own rolling stock in order to improve specific services where they see the need. All multiple-units in this category have numbers prefixed by a 9. Thus Class X 92100 is the 'privately owned' equivalent of Class X 2100. Units X 92101-X 92103 were built specially for the Pays de la Loire region in order to improve services from Nantes to Le Croisic. They usually work on this service, although they also appear on other regional services. With the electrification of the line to Le Croisic in 1986, they will probably cascade onto other lines. These units are identical to Class X 2100 except for their different seats and the livery of orange with pale grey bands. As can be seen from the photograph, they carry the name of the region in large letters above their windows. They also carry nameplates with the regional name, one of which can just be seen behind the open doors at the far end of X 92101, pictured here on Nantes depot. To add to the above three, X 2133 was purchased in 1982 by the Midi-Pyrénées region for services based on Toulouse and renumbered X 92104. This unit is in the same livery as Class X 2100 but carries nameplates showing the region's ownership.

Class X 2400

Car type: XABDP
Number series: X 2401-X 2478 (46)
Length: 27.73m (90ft 11in)
Weight: 43 tonnes
Seating: 12 first; 56 second
Usual formation: Single unit plus up to three trailers
Built by: Decauville/Renault/Saurer
Introduced: 1951-56

UIC power rating: 437kW (590hp)
Engine:
2x Renault 517G of 250kW (335hp) each (X 2401-2469)
2x Saurer BZDS-B of 255kW (340hp) each (X 2470-2478)
Transmission: Mechanical
Maximum speed: 120km/h (75mph)
Depots of allocation: RS, LI
Works responsible: Bordeaux
Livery: Red with cream window band

These units, whose throaty engine roar has animated the quiet Brittany countryside for many years, are now being withdrawn after over 30 years of stalwart service. The final nails in their coffin will be the arrival of Classes X 2200 and Z 9600 which will replace much of the class either directly or by a process of 'cascading' other stock into their place. At present they are still common all over Brittany and the Vendée (the area south of Nantes) and can be seen in smaller numbers in the Limoges, Périgueux and Bordeaux areas. Although not dissimilar to Class X 2800, their red and cream livery and the two 'eyes' on the front windows easily distinguish the class. The photograph shows unit X 2417 arriving at Rennes with a stopping train from Redon. In this case, the unit is towing two standard trailer cars although their number can vary from day to day according to traffic. There exist four different types of 'independent' trailer cars like the ones seen here, each differing according to their seating arrangements. A newer type has more recently been introduced, with a similar outline and livery to Class X 2100. These are used particularly with Classes X 2100 and X 2800.

Class X 2700 (RGP – Rame à Grand Parcours)

Car type:	XBD	XRABx
Number series:	X 2704-X 2719 (5)	XR 7701-XR 7726
Length:	26.63m (87ft 4in)	25.53m (83ft 9in)
Weight:	45 tonnes	32 tonnes
Seating:	48 second	21 first; 44 second

Usual formation: Two-car
Built by: De Dietrich/Renault
Introduced: 1954-55
UIC power rating: 437kW (590hp)
Engines: 2x Renault 517G of 250kW (335hp) each
Transmission: Mechanical
Maximum speed: 124km/h (77mph)
Depot of allocation: BX
Works responsible: No longer overhauled
Livery: Pale green with cream window band and aluminium trim *or* orange with pale grey bands at window level

These units are known as 'RGP2s' rather than by their class number. RGP, roughly translated, means 'long distance unit' and 2 denotes its twin engines compared with Classes X 2720 and X 2770 which have only one power unit. In fact, the class was built for prestige services on long, non-electrified cross-country routes but has been displaced onto more lowly tasks by the ETGs, RTGs and loco-hauled passenger trains. Unlike their single-engined equivalents which will be refurbished, the class is being withdrawn and will be extinct by 1987. Their decreasing sphere of action is based on Bordeaux and spreads out to Sarlat, Saintes and Limoges. They are particularly common on the route to Périgueux and it is probably here that they will work their last trains. In orange and grey livery they look rather similar to the RGP1s, and, indeed, work with the same trailer cars (see notes on X 2720/70). However, the power cars can be distinguished by their less streamlined front ends and the four front windows instead of five. The units remaining in green and cream livery are of particular interest as they are the only trains in normal service in France to carry these colours. Unfortunately, the effect cannot be seen on this black and white photograph of X 2713 on Bordeaux depot.

Classes X 2720 & X 2770 (RGP – Rame à Grand Parcours)

Car type:	XBD	XRABx
Number series:	X 2721-X 2738 (18) X 2771-X 2781 (11)	XR 7721-XR 7732 XR 7751-XR 7756 XR 7771-XR 7779
Length:	27.63m (90ft 8in) **R** 26.63m (87ft 4in) **U**	26.05m (85ft 5in) **R** 25.53m (83ft 9in) **U**
Weight:	[illegible] tonnes **R** 48 tonnes **U**	[illegible] tonnes **R** [illegible] **U**
Seating:	60 second **R** (X 2721-38) 56 second **R** (X 2771-81)	24 first **R** 52 second **R**

NB Seating capacities are only given for the refurbished versions as there are no less than seven different versions of the unrefurbished trailers.
R=refurbished **U**=unrefurbished

Permanent formation: Two-car
Built by: De Dietrich/SACM
Introduced: 1955-56
UIC power rating: 426kW (575hp)
Engine: MGO V12SH of 605kW (815hp)
Transmission: Hydro-mechanical
Maximum speed: 140km/h (87mph)
Depots of allocation: LY, MZ
Works responsible: Bordeaux
Livery: *Refurbished* – White with red window band and cab surround with dark grey roof, solebar and front end panel
Unrefurbished – Orange with dark grey roof and solebar and pale grey window band

RGP1 units are in very good condition for their age, and so SNCF has decided to give them a second refurbishment which will take them into the 21st century. The face-lift is quite dramatic, including interiors similar to the Z 2 series of electric units, automatic doors like those on Corail coaches, completely new cab units similar to those of Class X 2100 which make them the same at both ends and a striking new livery. Refurbished units can be used in multiple, whereas a second driver is needed for rakes of more than two unrefurbished units. The first few modernised units were used on the 'Alpazur', a summer-dated train between Grenoble and Marseille via the scenic foothills of the Alps, and on services from Nancy connecting with Rapide trains serving Paris.

RGP1 units have rather a chequered history. Both Classes X 2720 and X 2770 were built, like Class X 2700 as long distance express units, X 2770 being used on 'Trans Europ Express' services. As TEE routes were either abandoned or equipped with more modern stock, Class X 2770 was gradually deprived of its original role and Class X 2720 was also downgraded to more modest work. In the mid-1970s they were refurbished in a common programme and since then have been used in common, although there have remained differences in internal layouts. This is especially true for the trailer cars. The different groups of X 77XX trailers were, in fact, shared with Class X 2700. I have only grouped them as seen in the book out of convenience and this explains the irregularities in the numbers. Outwardly, the two RGP1 classes are identical. Power cars, like No X 2727, seen here on Metz depot, have a curved front end with five cab windows and look quite modern considering their age. Trailer cars have completely different front ends which are flatter, with either three windows, or as seen here on XR 7778, only two on the right and in the centre. It is clear that SNCF prefers to use the driving position in the trailer car as little as possible as most RGP formations one sees consist of two units with the power cars at the outer ends. The present operating sphere of the RGP1s is mainly in non-electrified mountainous areas, especially in the Vosges around Nancy and Epinal, and in the Alps to the east of Lyon, especially on the line to Bourg St Maurice.

Class X 2800

Car type: XABD
Number series: X 2801-X 2919 (118)
Length: 27.73m (90ft 11in)
Weight: 53 tonnes
Seating: 12 first; 62 second
X 2817/20/1/31/3/53/4/81/91, 2903/9/10 have 24 first, 50 second
Usual formation: Single unit plus up to three trailers

Built by: Decauville (X 2801-X 2816)
Renault (X 2817-X 2919)
Introduced: 1957-62
UIC power rating: 426kW (570hp)
Engines: MGO V12SH of 605kW (815hp)
Transmission: Hydro-mechanical
Maximum speed: 120km/h (75mph)
Depots of allocation: LI, LY, TE
Works responsible: Bordeaux
Livery: Mid blue with white window band and pale grey panel round cab windows and between side windows

These are the most powerful single units on the SNCF network which makes them perfectly suited to services on diesel lines in mountainous areas. They are known as 'Massif Central' units because of their wide use in that area, but are also used widely in the Alps and Jura. No X 2828 is seen here coupled to an X 4630 on a Grenoble–Lyon service, an 'under the wires' working that will soon give way to an electric unit. Identification of the class is moderately easy, the only similar units being Class X 2400 which are in red livery rather than blue. Units at work in the Massif Central can often be seen with independent trailer cars of Class XR 6000 which resemble Class X 2100 units. These were built specifically for work in that area at the same time as Class X 2800 was refurbished in the late 1970s.

Class X 3800

Car type: XBD or XABD
Number series: X 3801-X 4049 (50)
Length: 21.851m (71ft 8in)
Weight: 32 tonnes
Seating: 62 second (XBD) or 16 first; 32 second (XABD) 3864/7, 3931/42/3
Usual formation: Single unit plus one trailer if necessary
Built by: ANF/De Dietrich/Renault/Saurer

Introduced: 1950-61
UIC power rating: 205-232kW (273-310hp) depending on engine fitted
Engine:
Renault 517G of 250kW (335hp) 3801-35/61-91/3914-48/64-74
Saurer BZDS of 225kW (345hp) 3837-53/96-3900/94-4001/31/32
Renault 575 of 265kW (355hp) 3951/56/4013
Transmission: Mechanical
Maximum speed: 120km/h (75mph)
Depots of allocation: BX, MN, SE, NS, LP
Works responsible: No longer overhauled
Livery: Red below window level with cream above

These small, lightweight single units are known to French railwaymen and enthusiasts as 'Picassos' probably because of their strange, unbalanced outline produced by the driver's compartment which projects from one side of the roof. This was quite a common feature of French railcars in the past and was presumably done to free more space for passengers in the unit body. 'Picassos' are used on some of the most lightly loaded local stopping trains in France, particularly around Rouen and Caen, Reims and Charleville-Mézières and in the area between Nevers and Dijon. Surprisingly, they work one international service – between Charleville-Mézières and Dinant in Belgium. They are now being withdrawn quickly and will all disappear by 1989. Until then, enthusiasts have a few years in which to capture their distinctive outline on film in some of the most beautiful areas of France.

Few variations exist within the class and those which do are not obvious to the casual observer. As the table of details shows, three different engines have been used to power the class. The majority of units are second class only, but a few are fitted with both first and second class seats. All five remaining such examples are allocated to Nevers depot. The example on page 95 is second class only No X 3964 which was photographed at Sotteville depot.

Three of the class have been converted for special use and may remain in service a little longer than normal service units. No X 3896, which is shown below at its usual base, Noisy-le-Sec, and X 3900 were converted in 1972 into inspection saloons with special seating, eating and sleeping (!) facilities. As well as their livery of pale green lined in white, they can be distinguished from normal 'Picassos' by their large double front windows and two additional headlights at roof level. No X 3997, which acts as a rolling laboratory for measurement concerned with signalling and telecommunications is similar to these former two in having two large front windows, but has no high level headlamps and is painted in 'Corail' livery of pale and dark grey lined in orange.

Classes X 4300 & X 4500 EAD – Eléments Automoteurs Doubles

Car type:	XBD	XRABx
Number series:	X 4301-X 4451 (145) X 4501-X 4626 (125)	XR 8301-XR 8451 (145) XR 8501-XR 8739 (239)
Length:	21.24m (69ft 8in)	21.24m (69ft 8in)
Weight:	35-36 tonnes	23 tonnes
Seating:	60 second	XR 8300: 12 first 69 second XR 8500: 24 first 49 second

Usual formation: Two-car
Built by: ANF/Saurer/Poyaud
Introduced: 1963-70
UIC power rating: 295kW (400hp)
Engine: Poyaud of 320kW (430hp) X 4300
Saurer SDHR of 320kW (430hp) X 4500
Transmission: Mechanical
Maximum speed: 120km/h (75mph)
Depots of allocation: TS, NT, MZ (X 4300) LU, ME, SE (X 4500)
Works responsible: Le Mans
Livery: Red with cream band around windows and dark grey around cab windows and between side windows

Together with very similar Class X 4630 which has hydraulic transmission, and X 4750 which has a higher maximum speed, these two classes form the mainstay of SNCF's DMU fleet. As such they can be seen almost anywhere in France, except in the south-western corner, mainly on local stopping trains, but also on some less important expresses. Although easily enough distinguished from other units by their three window front end and corrugated sides, there is no clear way of telling the difference between Classes X 4300 and X 4500 as they are identical except for their engine. There is also no visible difference between these two and Class X 4630 despite the latter's different transmission. In fact, trailer cars of Classes XR 8300 and XR 8500 are mixed freely between the three classes, and thus the grouping above is only for convenience. However, formations tend to be quasi-permanent, only changing in case of a major incident or significant change in traffic patterns. All units in this group are known as 'Caravelles' to railwaymen. No X 4304 is seen below, being cleaned on Nantes depot.

Classes X 4630 & X 94630

	XBD	XRABx
Car type:	XBD	XRABx
Number series:	X 4630-X 4742 (143) X 94630	Used with XR 8300 or XR 8500 XR 98630
Length:	21.24m (69ft 8in)	21.24m (69ft 8in)
Weight:	39 tonnes	24 tonnes
Seating:	60 second	24 first 49 second

Permanent information: Two-car
Built by: ANF/Saurer
Introduced: 1974-77
UIC power rating: 295kW (400hp)
Engine: Saurer SDHR of 320kW (430hp)
Transmission: Hydraulic
Maximum speed: 100km/h ([illegible])
Depots of allocation: LY, LU, NT, NS (X 4630) ME (X 94630)
Works responsible: Le Mans
Livery: Red with cream band around windows and dark grey round cab windows and between side windows (also see below)

Class X 4630 is very similar to Classes X 4300 & X 4500 except for the use of hydraulic transmission and that the last few members of the class have cast SNCF symbols on the front end like Class X 4750. Except for a small number, all are allocated to the Sud Est region at Nevers and Lyon Vaise and cover almost all the non-electrified lines of the region. Between late 1985 and mid 1987, 21 of the class are to be refurbished, with improved interiors, for the 'Pays de la Loire' region. They will carry a white livery with a green band at roof level and a blue band at waist level and work from Nantes depot. X 94630 is an identical unit which has been purchased by Cannes public transport authority to work the recently reopened three-mile branch to Ranguin. SNCF fare levels and tickets are not applicable on this service, and, indeed, the unit is fitted with bus-type ticket cancellors. The unit, which is seen here at Cannes has the striking livery of bright blue, with a yellow band at window level. It is maintained at Marseille, and replaced by an X 4500 unit when at the depot.

Class X 4750

Car type:	XBD	XRABx
Number series:	X 4750-X 4796 (47)	XR 8750-XR 8796 (47)
Length:	21.24m (69ft 8in)	21.24m (69ft 8in)
Weight:	39 tonnes	24 tonnes
Seating:	60 second (4750-89) 47 second (4790-96)	24 first (all) 49 second (4750-89) 36 second (4790-96)

Permanent formation: Two-car
Built by: ANF/Saurer/Creusot-Loire
Introduced: 1977-81
UIC power rating: 440kW (600hp)
Engine: Saurer
Transmission: Hydraulic
Maximum speed: 140km/h (87mph)
Depots of allocation: SE, MZ
Works responsible: Le Mans
Livery: Red with cream band around windows and dark grey round cab windows and between side windows (see below, X 4790-96)

Class X 4750 is a further development of the 'standard' two-car diesel multiple-unit following on from X 4300, X 4500 and X 4630. The main advances on previous designs are its greater power and higher maximum speed, making it possible to be used on semi-fast expresses. Visually, there is little to distinguish X 4750-X 4789 from the previous classes except for the cast SNCF symbol on the front end where before there were transfers. This is clear on this view of X 4763, with X 8763 leading, on Sotteville depot.

The final seven units of the class (X 4790-X 4796), although mechanically the same, are significantly different from Nos X 4750-89, as they were built as part of a plan to improve services on the minor main line from Paris Montparnasse to Granville. These units are fitted with lower density seating of the individual type used in 'Z2' electric units. For the observer, they are immediately recognisable by their livery of orange relieved by a pale grey window band and dark grey around the cab windows with double red lines above the windows and a red cross design on the front end between the headlights. All units are named after towns along the line and carry plates at the opposite ends advertising the participation of the Normandie region. The units are mainly used on the Granville line but sometimes are found interworking elsewhere on Sotteville Class X 4750 diagrams.

Class X 94750
(RAP – Rames Automotrices Postales)

Car type:	XP	XRPx
Number series:	X 94750-X 94757 (8)	XR 98750-XR 98757 (8)
Length:	21.24m (69ft 8in)	21.24m (69ft 8in)
Weight:	39 tonnes	23 tonnes
Seating:	—	—

Permanent information: Two-car
Built by: ANF/Saurer
Introduced: 1978-79
UIC power rating: 440kW (600hp)
Engine: Saurer

Transmission: Hydraulic
Maximum speed: 140km/h (87mph)
Depots of allocation: SE
Works responsible: Le Mans
Livery: Maroon with a wide cream band and pale grey round cab windows

This is a special version of Class X 4750 which has no passenger accommodation having internal space for transporting post instead. They are owned by the French post office and are used from Paris to Caen, Rouen and Lille. This means that the majority of their work is done 'under the wires'. Below, X 94755 is seen stabled between workings. The units are easily identified not only by their lack of windows but also by their distinctive maroon and cream livery which is carried by no other class.

Class X 4900
EAT – (Eléments Automoteurs Triples)

Car type:	XBD	XRAB
Number series:	X 4901-X 4926 (26)	XR 8901-XR 8913 (13)
Length:	21.24m (69ft 8in)	20.75m (68ft 1in)
Weight:	39 tonnes	28 tonnes
Seating:	47 second	32 first 28 second

Permanent formation: Three-car (XBD+XRAB+XBD)
Built by: ANF/Saurer
Introduced: 1975-77
UIC power rating: 590kW (800hp) for whole unit
Engine: Saurer SHDR of 320kW (430hp)
Transmission: Hydraulic
Maximum speed: 140km/h (87mph)
Depots of allocation: SE, ME
Works responsible: Le Mans
Livery: Light blue with white window band and pale grey round cab windows

These are the only three-car diesel units on the SNCF network, and are recognisable by their blue and white livery which is similar to that applied to Classes X 2100 and X 2800. Power cars are mechanically identical to those of Class X 4630, but seating is to a lower density and is more luxurious like that in units X 4790-96. Class X 4900 workings are confined to two particular areas: Sotteville units work between Caen and Rouen, Le Mans and Rennes whilst Marseille sets are concentrated on the lines from Briançon to Marseille and Livron. In both cases, these are generally semi-express trains, which this class is particularly suited to. In the illustration unit X 4914+XR 8907+X 4913 is seen on Sotteville depot.

Class Z 100

Car type: ZB
Number series: Z 102-Z 118 (14)
Length:
14.904m (48ft 11in)
14.384m (47ft 2in) for ex-trailers:
Z 105/11/3/6/7/8
Weight: 32 tonnes or 28 tonnes for ex-trailers
Seating: 40 second
Formation: Single unit with trailers if necessary
Built by: Cardes & Co/SNCF
Introduced: 1908-09
UIC power rating: 265kW (355hp)
Maximum speed: 55km/h (34mph)
Nominal supply voltage: 850V dc Third rail
Depot of allocation: VV
Works responsible: Béziers
Livery: Red with yellow from window bottoms upwards. Now appearing in yellow lined out in red

These units work on the remarkable metre-gauge line from Villefranche-le-Conflent to La Tour-de-Carol in the eastern Pyrenees. The trains are affectionately known as the 'Canary' or 'Little Yellow Train' by the locals and tourists, and the railway is called the 'Cerdagne line' by SNCF, after the name of the region it passes through. The line is amazing for its tortuosity and steepness as well as for its scenery and, of course, for its rolling stock, which is now over 75 years old. There are two types of power car, which are, in fact, very similar. The original power cars, like Z 108 pictured here, have passenger doors near one end, while those power cars which have been converted from trailers have the access doors in the middle. Units operate singly in the off-peak season or in pairs with a ZR 20000 trailer car between in the winter and summer peak seasons. SNCF have recently considered replacing these units but, instead, have decided to have them refurbished, with improved cabs, suspension, seating and soundproofing. Units are at present passing through Béziers works and will receive the new livery as they are refurbished. Enthusiasts visiting France are advised to take a trip on this line if they do nothing else – it's quite an experience!

Class Z 600

Car type: ZAB
Number series: Z 601-Z 608 (8)
Length: 18.2m (59ft 8in)
Weight: 40 tonnes
Seating: 8 first; 34 second
Formation: Single unit with trailers if necessary (see below)
Built by: Decauville/Oerlikon
Introduced: 1958
UIC power rating: 885kW (1,190hp)
Maximum speed: 70km/h (43mph)
Nominal supply voltage: 750V dc Third rail
Depot of allocation: SB
Works responsible: Oullins
Livery: Silver-grey with orange window band and solebar

Class Z 600 are third-rail, metre-gauge single units which work on the line between Saint Gervais and Vallorcine in the Savoy Alps. This line can be found in the Guinness Book of Records as it is the steepest in the world to be worked by adhesion alone. It is not surprising, then, that such small single units pack almost 1,200hp. The units work singly in the low season, but in summer, and especially during the winter sports season (the line passes through Chamonix), trailer cars of Class ZR 20600 are added between power cars to give three-car or five-car formations. A three-car train, with Z 608 nearest the camera, can be seen here leaving Saint Gervais. Power cars are very similar to trailers, the power cars being recognisable by their roof-mounted cooling equipment and single central entrance door. The 'Savoie' line, as it is known, has, like the 'Cerdagne' line, numerous other powered vehicles, including three snowploughs, for maintaining the line. It is not intended to cover these sundry vehicles in this book as their minor importance would not merit the amount of space needed to describe them fully.

Class Z 5100

Car type:	ZBD	ZRB	ZRABx
Number series:	Z 5101-5182 (81)	ZR 25101-25176 (75)	ZR 15101-15182 (81)
Length:	22.85m (74ft 11in)	22.4m (73ft 6in)	22.85m (74ft 11in)
Weight:	57 tonnes	35 tonnes	37 tonnes
Seating:	72 second	82 second	24 first 44 second

Permanent formation:
Three-car (Z 5101-Z 5176)
(ZBD+ZRB+ZRABx)
Two-car (Z 5177-Z 5182)
(ZBD+ZRABx)
Built by: Carel Fouché/MTE
Introduced: 1954-57
UIC power rating:
790kW (1,060hp) Z 5101-Z 5176
495kW (665hp) Z 5177-Z 5182
Maximum speed: 120km/h (75mph)

Pantograph type: Faiveley G diamond
Nominal supply voltage:
1500V dc Overhead (Z 5101-Z 5176)
750V dc Third rail (Z 5177-Z 5182)
Depots of allocation: MR, VE, TC
(Z 5177-Z 5182 at SL)
Works responsible: Vitry
Livery: Stainless steel with frontal SNCF roundel on red background

Now the oldest standard gauge EMUs on SNCF, Class Z 5100s have seen great changes in utilisation in the past five years. Whilst being gradually displaced from their traditional role on suburban services out of Paris Lyon and Montparnasse, they have been transferred to less intensive work on local stopping trains on the Orléans-Bordeaux and Limoges lines. Known as 'Budds', they now present a rather low standard of ride and comfort and are much noisier than more modern EMUs. They can be identified by their small front windows compared with later types, and by the diamond pantograph. All units, like Z 5124, seen here at Villeneuve St Georges, have the last three digits of their number painted on the front end. In 1985, six of these units, Z 5177-Z 5182, were converted to work off 750V dc third rail for use on the line from Puteaux to Issy Plaine, in the western Paris suburbs. This is the last standard gauge, third-rail line in France. Little outward difference exists between these and standard units, except that they have had the centre coach and pantograph removed and third-rail pick-up shoes fitted.

Class Z 5300

Car type:	ZBD	ZRB	ZRABx
Number series:	Z 5301-Z 5445 (144)	ZR 25301-25597 (288)	ZR 15301-15445 (144)
Length:	25.8m (84ft 7in) Z 5301-5359	25.6m (84ft 0in) Z 25301-25418	25.8m (84ft 7in) Z 15301-15359
	25.925m (85ft 4in) Z 5360-5445	25.85m (84ft 9in) Z 25419-25597	25.925m (85ft 4in) Z 15360-15445
Weight:	62 tonnes	30 tonnes	32 tonnes
Seating:	87 second	107 second	46 first 38 second

Permanent formation: Four-car (ZBD+ZRB+ZRB+ZRABx)
Built by: Carel Fouché/MTE/Fives-Lille/Oerlikon
Introduced: 1965-75
UIC power rating: 1,180kW (1,585hp)
Maximum speed: 120km/h (75mph)
Pantograph type: Faiveley AM18B single arm
Nominal supply voltage: 1,500V dc
Depots of allocation: VE, PS
Works responsible: Vitry
Livery: Stainless steel

This large class works in two main areas at present: on suburban services out of Paris Lyon and on RER line C from the Versailles area through Invalides and Austerlitz low level to several destinations in the southern suburbs of Paris. Although the majority of their work is, at present, on line C, the delivery of Class Z 5600 and then Z 8800 will allow more to be transferred to Paris Lyon and Montparnasse services, thus displacing Z 5100 units and some loco-powered stock. Like Class Z 5100, these units are finished in bare stainless steel but can be recognised by their much larger, squarer front windows. Several differences exist between the first and second batches, though. The first 59, like No Z 5313, seen here at Villeneuve St Georges, have slightly shorter coaches, round SNCF symbols on the front, and side windows which are grouped together and enclosed in a raised surround. Like members of Class Z 5100, the last three figures of the number are carried on the front end.

The second batch, like Z 5368, photographed above at Choisy-le-Roi (near Orly airport), look more modern as they have the lettered SNCF sign on the front and individual side windows, each with a visible rubber seal. The final 52 units of this batch, Z 5394-Z 5445 will be retained for some time on RER line C, and have received improved interiors and seating. As they pass through works they are also being fitted with indicator panels on the cab roof to show a four letter code (YETI on this photograph of Z 5426 at Juvisy) which indicates the stopping pattern of the train for waiting passengers. This idea has been incorporated in the design of new units of Classes Z 5600, Z 8100 and Z 8800 which also work on the RER system.

Class Z 5600

Car type:	ZB	ZRB	ZRAB
Number series:	Z 5601-Z 5704 (104)	ZR 25601-up	ZR 35601-up
Length:	25.1m (82ft 4in)	24.28 (79ft 8in)	24.28m (79ft 8in)
Weight:	65 tonnes	41 tonnes	41 tonnes
Seating:	115 second	168 second	70 first 82 second

Formation:
Four-car (ZB+ZRB+ZRAB+ZB)
PS version (5633-5704)
Five-car (ZB+ZRB+ZRB+ZRAB+ZB)
VE version (5601-5632)
Built by: ANF/CIMT/Oerlikon/Alsthom
Introduced: 1983-85
UIC power rating: 1,400kW (1,880hp) per power car (3,760hp per unit)
Maximum speed: 140km/h (87mph)
Pantograph type: Faiveley AM65BU single arm
Nominal supply voltage: 1,500V dc
Depots of allocation: VE, PS
Works responsible: Vitry
Livery: White with dark blue band between side windows, red doors and frontal panel and dark grey roof

Although there have been locomotive-powered double-deck trains on French railways since the 1880s (!) this is the first class of double-deck units. They were made necessary in order to increase the capacity of suburban trains without increasing platform lengths and because the steep banks out of Paris Lyon and Austerlitz low-level stations have proven too much for a single locomotive with an eight-coach train. Rather than tie up two locomotives at once, SNCF preferred to design double-deck power cars. The units can easily be told from locomotive-powered double-deck trains which have a different front end design and are painted in yellow and white. For these units an earlier front end colour scheme has since been superseded by a scheme in which the blue window band stops at the cabside window and the front end is covered by a panel of dark blue at the top and red at the bottom, all surrounded by a black band. This is carried by Z 5657 (below). Double-deck units have the generic name 'Z2N' and a bi-current version of this class, numbered Z 8801-Z 8896 started to be delivered in late 1985 for use on services on RER line C which will be extended via a new line to the north-western suburbs of Paris which are electrified at 25kV ac. Trailer cars are, at present, mixed up and shared with Class Z 8800. A second batch of bi-current units will be ordered later when RER line D is created by linking the suburban lines out of Paris Lyon and Nord in 1989.

Classes Z 6000 & Z 6100

Car type:	ZBD	ZRB	ZRABx
Number series:	Z 6006-Z 6009 (4) Z 6101-Z 6185 (81)	ZR 26006-26009 ZR 26101-26185	ZR 16006-16009 ZR 16101-16185
Length:	25.5m (83ft 8in)	23.8 (78ft 1in)	25.15m (82ft 6in)
Weight:	34-35 tonnes	27-37 tonnes	29-31 tonnes
Seating:	79 second	107 second	36 first 51 second

Permanent formation: Three-car (ZBD+ZRB+ZRABx)
Built by: Carel Fouché/Alsthom/SW/CEM
Introduced:
1960-61 (Z 6006-Z 6009)
1965-71 (Z 6101-Z 6185)
UIC power rating:
690kW (925hp) Z 6006-Z 6009
615kW (825hp) rest

Maximum speed: 120km/h (75mph)
Pantograph type: Faiveley AM11 single arm
Nominal supply voltage: 25kV ac 50Hz
Depot of allocation: LE
Works responsible: La Folie
Livery: Stainless steel

These two Classes were the first 25kV ac units on the SNCF network and were built for the electrification of suburban lines out of Paris Gare du Nord. They are used on all lines out of Paris Nord, except to Roissy and Mitry, and work as far north as Amiens. They are moderately similar in design to dc units Class Z 5300, but have several differences including lower positioning of the windows and coupler on the front end and different door and window spacing along the sides. For the reader, a greater difficulty will arise in telling the difference between these units and locomotive-powered stainless steel suburban stock used in the same area. Differences between units within these two classes are easier to identify. Units of Class Z 6000 can be distinguished by the 'winged' SNCF roundel on the front end, and, less obviously, by the lack of a roof-mounted equipment box between the pantograph and the long central roof box. Both of these features are easily seen in the photograph of unit Z 6008 at La Chapelle depot.

Of the Z 6100s, two groups are distinguishable visibly. All these units have a non-winged SNCF roundel, but Z 6101-20 are more like Class Z 6000 in having their side windows grouped in threes, enclosed by a raised surround. Z 6121-85 on the other hand, have individually sealed side windows. A comparison of the two styles can be made between Nos Z 6102 above, and Z 6122 below. Notice that all these units carry the last three digits of their number on their sides and in the cab window. Although visibly identical there exist electrical differences between the batches Z 6121-49 and Z 6150-85. Four of the latter batch are missing as they were sold to Luxembourg Railways (CFL). CFL also has some two-car versions of this class.

Class Z 6300

Car type:	ZBD	ZRAB	ZRBx
Number series:	Z 6301-Z 6335 (35)	ZR 26301-26335	ZR 16301-16335
Length:	20.75m (68ft 1in)	18.825m (61ft 9in)	20.525m (67ft 4in)
Weight:	51 tonnes	26 tonnes	28 tonnes
Seating:	21 second	40 first 21 second	70 second

Permanent formation: Three-car (ZBD+ZRAB+ZRBx)
Built by: Carel Fouché/Alsthom/SW/CEM
Introduced: 1967-70
UIC power rating: 615kW (825hp)
Maximum speed: 120km/h (75mph)
Pantograph type: Faiveley AM11 single arm
Nominal supply voltage: 25kV ac 50Hz
Depot of allocation: AS
Works responsible: La Folie
Livery: Stainless steel

This class is an adaptation of the Z 6100 design, specially built for the tight curvature and high platforms of certain suburban lines out of Paris St Lazare. It can be seen from the illustration of Z 6306 at Achères that there are only two window bays between sets of doors as against three on Class Z 6100. The reduced coach length was partially compensated for by the building-in of a half-width cab, thus giving enough extra space for two seats. These units also have a special device for raising and lowering the step height for different platform levels. Z 6300 units are used on services to Cormeilles-en-Parisis, Conflans-Ste-Honorine, Pontoise and Mantes-la-Jolie via the Conflans route.

Class Z 6400

Car type:	ZAD	ZB	ZRB
Number series:	Z 6401-6549 (odd)	Z 6402-6550 (even)	ZR 26401-26550
Length:	22.7m (74ft 5in)	22.7m (74ft 5in)	22.39m (73ft 5in)
Weight:	58 tonnes	58 tonnes	28 tonnes
Seating:	72 first	88 second	102 second

Permanent formation: Four-car (ZAD+ZRB+ZRB+ZB)
Built by: Carel Fouché/Alsthom/De Dietrich/Oerlikon
Introduced: 1976-79
UIC power rating: 1,180kW (1,585hp) per power car (3,170hp per unit)
Maximum speed: 120km/h (75mph)
Pantograph type: Faiveley AM18U single arm
Nominal supply voltage: 25kV ac 50Hz
Depot of allocation: SL
Works responsible: La Folie
Livery: Stainless steel with blue band at window level and yellow headlight panel on front end

These units were built in connection with suburban electrification (or re-electrification) schemes out of Paris Nord and St Lazare, but are now concentrated on the latter. Their high power rating is needed for fast acceleration because of short inter-station distances. They were the first units in the Paris area, and indeed on SNCF, to be one-man operated. Z 6401-Z 6440 and Z 6525-Z 6550 are used on trains to Cergy, Pontoise and Bois-Colombes as they have variable door step heights like Class Z 6300. The remainder of the class, Nos Z 6441-Z 6524, are used on the Versailles Rive Droite and St Nom-la-Breteche services where all platforms are the high type. This view shows Z 6444 (and Z 6443) at Puteaux, near La Défense in western Paris, with a stopping service to St Lazare. Again, the unit has the last part of its number in the cab window.

Class Z 7100

	ZABD	ZRBD
Car type:	ZABD	ZRBD
Number series:	Z 7101-7133 (32)	ZR 27101-27135
Length:	26.13m (85ft 8in)	22.68m (74ft 5in)
Weight:	55 tonnes	24 tonnes
Seating:	12 first 58 second	76 second

Formation:
Four-car (Z + ZR + ZR + ZRx) 7101-20
Two-car (Z + ZRx) 7121-33

Built by: Decauville/De Dietrich/Oerlikon
Introduced: 1960-62
UIC power rating: 940kW (1,260hp)
Maximum speed: 130km/h (81mph)
Pantograph type: Faiveley AM11 single arm
Nominal supply voltage: 1,500V dc
Depots of allocation: VX (Four-car), AN (Two-car)
Works responsible: Oullins
Livery: Red with cream window band. Refurbished units are mid-blue with white window band and pale grey round cab windows and between side windows

Class Z 7100, known as 'Zezettes' to railwaymen, are at present being refurbished, and so exact details of formations are not forthcoming and explanations are complicated. Originally, power cars were treated like single diesel units in that they could be coupled with a variable number of trailer cars to a maximum of three. Along with refurbishment, it was decided to make permanently-coupled sets in the future. The first batch, Nos Z 7101-20, would be four-car formations to be used on suburban services around Lyon. The second, Z 7121-33, which are fitted with rheostatic brakes, would be two-car and would perform a variety of duties including services on the mountainous Béziers-Neussargues route. Units have already been regrouped at Vénissieux and Avignon and, like Z 7103 seen here at Lyon Part Dieu with a train for St Etienne, are already in their proposed formations.

ZRABD	ZRBDx	ZRABDx
ZR 27201-27212	ZR 17101-17120	ZR 17201-17208
22.68m (74ft 5in)	22.68m (74ft 5in)	22.68m (74ft 5in)
24 tonnes	24 tonnes	25 tonnes
24 first	76 second	24 first
34 second		34 second

The changes made to the refurbished units include new cab units, the removal of one of the two pantographs, a much improved interior with seats similar to the 'Z2' units and, of course, the new blue & white livery. At the same time, the power car will be turned round, putting the pantograph at the back end instead of the front. In order for the desired formations to be possible, additional trailer cars will have to be fitted with cabs. And in view of the passenger capacities projected, 24 first/232 second for a four-car, and 12 first/111 second in a two-car, internal trailer car layouts will have to be completely revised. In the meantime, the above car descriptions refer to unrefurbished units. The outward result of the modifications can be judged from the photograph of Z 7101 next to unrefurbished Z 7123 in the following illustration.

Class Z 7300 & Z 97300

Car type:	ZABD	ZRBx
Number series:	Z 7301-7373 (73) Z 97301-97304 (4)	ZR 17301-17373 (73) ZR 917301-917304 (4)
Length:	25.1m (82ft 4in)	25.1m (82ft 4in)
Weight:	64 tonnes	40 tonnes
Seating:	24 first 43 second	84 second

Permanent formation: Two-car (ZABD+ZRBx)
Built by:
7301-7335 Francorail/MTE
7336-7352 Carel Fouché
7353-7373 De Dietrich
Introduced: 1980-85
UIC power rating: 1,220kW (1,640hp)
Maximum speed: 160km/h (99mph)
Pantograph type: Faiveley AM 10D single arm
Nominal supply voltage: 1,500V dc
Depots of allocation: BX, TS, ME
Works responsible: Oullins
Livery: Dark blue with red doors and front ends and grey roof, solebar and cab sides (see below for 97303/4)

Class Z 7300 is the first of a group of standardised electric units with the generic name of 'Z2'. These units were conceived for semi-fast and stopping services on electrified lines, and their high power/weight ratio gives them extremely good acceleration. Two different seat configurations are possible for the 'Z2's. Z 7300 have the higher density 'omnibus' ie stopping services, configuration. They are used over much of the Sud Ouest region south of Tours and along the Toulouse-Marseille transversal route and its branches. Here, unit Z 7358, trailer car at the front, is seen on Tours depot.

Two batches of two Z 7300s have been bought by 'third-parties' and are numbered Z 97301-4. The first two, Z 97301/2, were paid for by the Midi-Pyrénées region and carry nameplates to illustrate the fact. Otherwise, they are identical to the remainder of the class as can be seen in the photograph of No Z 97302 at Bordeaux. Z 97303/4 are owned by the Languedoc-Roussillon region and have a particularly colourful livery. They are in white with bands of orange, green and blue along the sides and the letters TLR (Transports de Languedoc-Roussillon) on the front ends.

Class Z 7500

Car type:	ZABD	ZRBx
Number series:	Z 7501-7515 (15)	ZR 17501-17515
Length:	25.1m (82ft 4in)	25.1m (82ft 4in)
Weight:	63 tonnes	40 tonnes
Seating:	32 first 32 second	76 second

Permanent formation: Two car (ZABD + ZRBx)
Built by: Alsthom/MTE
Introduced: 1982-83
UIC power rating: 1,220kW (1,640hp)
Maximum speed: 160km/h (99mph)

Pantograph type: Faiveley AM100 single arm
Nominal supply voltage: 1,500V dc
Depot of allocation: ME
Works responsible: Oullins
Livery: Dark blue with red doors and front ends and grey roof, solebar and cab sides

Class Z 7500 is the 1,500V dc, 'express' version of the standard 'Z2' unit design. As such they have more widely spaced seating than the Z 7300s and more first class accommodation. Otherwise, they are identical. Their main duties are along the main Marseille-Lyon-Dijon route on expresses stopping at the main stations. They also reach Sens on the Dijon-Paris line. In the photograph, Z 7315 is found a little off the beaten track, at Villefranche-Vernet-les-Bains in the foothills of the eastern Pyrenees.

Class Z 8100

Car type:	ZBD	ZRB	ZRAB
Number series:	Z 8101-8340 (240)	ZR 28101-28339 (odd)	ZR 28102-28340 (even)
Length:	26.08m (85ft 7in)	26m (85ft 3in)	26m (85ft 3in)
Weight:	56 tonnes	48 tonnes	48 tonnes
Seating:	72 second	84 second	32 first 52 second

Permanent formation: Four-car (ZBD+ZRB+ZRAB+ZBD)
Built by: Société Franco-Belge/ANF/Oerlikon
Introduced: 1980-84
UIC power rating:
Under 1,500V dc: 1,240kW (1,665hp) per power car
Under 25kV ac: 1,260kW (1,695hp) per power car
Maximum speed: 140km/h (87mph)
Pantograph type:
dc Faiveley AM18B single arm
ac Faiveley AM18U single arm
Nominal supply voltages: 1,500V dc & 25kV ac 50Hz
Depots of allocation: LE & Massy Palaiseau (RATP)
Works responsible: Massy Palaiseau
Livery: White with dark blue band at window level, red doors and front panel and grey solebar

Known as 'MI79' stock, these units were built for the Paris 'Interconnection' in which RER line B between Chatelet and St Remy lès Chevreuse was joined to the SNCF line from Gare du Nord to Roissy airport and Mitry Claye. This explains both the need for dual current units and the joint ownership of the class. Although the SNCF units are allocated to La Chapelle depot, they are not actually maintained there, being treated at Mitry for minor complaints or at Massy-Palaiseau for major incidents. The design is very distinctive, as is the livery. With their restricted zone of operation they should be easily recognisable. The photograph shows No Z 8303 (and Z 8304) at La Plaine Voyageurs. Notice that the pantographs are carried on the central trailer cars and that the unit is displaying the code 'KHOL' which indicates the stopping pattern of the train as on Classes Z 5300 & Z 5600. At present, units of MI84 stock a reduced cost version of Z 8100 are being introduced on RER line A. This has less comfortable seats and greatly modernised electronics. However, none has yet been delivered to SNCF.

Classes Z 9500 & Z 99500

Car type:	ZABD	ZRBx
Number series:	Z 9501-9518 (18) Z 99501/2 (2)	ZR 19501-19518 ZR 919501/2
Length:	25.1m (82ft 4in)	25.1m (82ft 4in)
Weight:	65 tonnes	40 tonnes
Seating:	32 first 33 second	76 second

Permanent formation: Two car (ZABD+ZRBx)
Built by: Alsthom/MTE
Introduced: 1982-83
UIC power rating: 1,200kW (1,610hp)
Maximum speed: 160km/h (99mph)

Pantograph type:
dc AM18B single arm
ac AM18U single arm
Nominal supply voltages: 1,500V dc & 25kV ac 50Hz
Depots of allocation: VX
Works responsible: Oullins
Livery: Dark blue with red doors and front ends and grey roof, solebar and cab sides

Class Z 9500 is the 'express', dual-current version of the 'Z2' design. As such, these units are similar to Class Z 7500 but have equipment for operating off 25kV ac including a pantograph on the trailer car. This can be seen in the photograph of Z 9507 at Vénissieux depot, with trailer ZR 19507 leading. The majority of the class are used on service between Lyon and Geneva/Evian. Trains are formed of two or three units which divide or join at Bellegarde. Most of the remainder work together with Z 99501/2 on the Dijon-Besançon-Belfort line. Z 99501/2 were bought by the Bourgogne-Franche Comté regional council and are identical to the rest of the class. Entering service at present is Class Z 9600, the 'omnibus' dual-current version of the 'Z2s'. These units will be employed on services on the Le Mans-Rennes and Nantes axes and will replace DMUs and gas turbine units on services around Lyon.

Classes T 1000 & T 1500 (ETG – Elément à Turbine à Gaz)

Car type:	TB	TRA	TRB	TBD
Number series:	T 1001-1014 (14)	TR 21001-14	TR51001-14	T 1501-1514
Former numbers:	X 4801-4810	XR 8701-8710	X 8801-8810	X 4701-4710
Length:	22.84m (74ft 11in)	20.75m (68ft 1in)	20.75m (68ft 1in)	22.84m (74ft 11in)
Weight:	42 tonnes	28 tonnes	33 tonnes	44 tonnes
Engine:	Turmo IIIF1 of 820kW (1,100hp)	—	—	Saurer SDHR of 320kW (430hp)
Transmission:	Hydrodynamic	—	—	Mechanical
Seating:	44 second	56 first	54 second	48 second

Permanent formation: Four-car (TB+TRA+TRB+TBD)
Built by: ANF/SNCF/Turboméca/Saurer
Introduced: 1969-72
UIC power rating: 1,031kW (1,390hp)
Maximum speed: 160km/h (99mph)
Depot of allocation: LY, VX
Works responsible: Le Mans
Livery: Orange with white bands above and below window line

These units are a surprising combination of a gas turbine power car, Nos T 1001-1514, two trailer cars and a diesel power car, Nos T 1501-1514. The gas turbine engine used was developed from a helicopter engine, whilst the diesel equipment is basically the same as that in the X 4300-X 4900 units. The class has been very successful wherever it has worked. At present, workings are changing as the units are replaced by electric motive power in their traditional 'fief' of the Lyon-Grenoble/Chambéry lines although they remain on the Geneva-Grenoble-Valence route. The first new services to be taken up have been the Metz-Dijon-Clermont Ferrand summer-dated service and Nevers-Dijon. Others are still to be specified. The units are similar to Class T 2000 but can be distinguished by the headlight on the cab roof, corrugated body sides and their different colour scheme. Here, T 1004 (with T 1504) is seen at Vénissieux depot.

Class T 2000
(RTG – Rame à Turbine à Gaz)

Car type:	TBD	TRA	TRBr	TRAB
Number series:	T 2001-2082 (78)	TR 22001-41	TR 52001-41	TR 42001-41
Length:	26.23m (86ft 0in)	25.51m (83ft 8in)	25.51m (83ft 8in)	25.51m (83ft 8in)
Weight:	64 tonnes	37 tonnes	42 tonnes	38 tonnes
Seating:	48 second	60 first	68 second	29 first 40 second

Permanent formation: Five-car (TBD+TRA+TRBr+TRAB+TBD)
Built by: ANF/Turboméca/Voith/MTE
Introduced: 1972-76
UIC power rating: 1,910kW (2,560hp)

Engines:
Turmo XII of 1,200kW (1,610hp) (uneven numbers)
Turmo IIIF1 of 820kW (1,100hp) (even numbers)

Transmission: Hydrodynamic
Maximum speed: 160km/h (99mph)
Depots of allocation: VX, CN
Works responsible: Le Mans
Livery: Orange with light grey roof, window band, solebar and frontal bands

These units were the 'stars' of the SNCF fleet when first introduced – before the TGV age. Originally fitted with two Turmo IIIF1 turbines per unit, they received the more powerful Turmo XII in their odd numbered power cars in a recent refit. Now, units often run with only the more powerful turbine running, except on starting and when making up time lost, in order to save fuel. RTGs are readily identifiable by their smooth outline and bright livery. They are allocated to just two depots and work singly or in pairs. Vénissieux units operate mainly on the Lyon-Strasbourg and Lyon-Bordeaux cross-country services while Caen units operate most of the fastest trains on the Paris-Caen-Cherbourg route and on Caen-Tours. Caen-based RTGs also work on the Nord region from Paris Nord to Boulogne (Aeroglisseurs) and Hirson. The photograph shows Nos T 2064 & T 2063 *Boulogne-sur-Mer* at Cherbourg.

Classes TGV 23000 & TGV 33000

Throughout the 1960s and 1970s SNCF was experimenting with high-speed rail travel. Traffic on the Paris-Dijon-Lyon route was continually increasing for both passenger and freight. Predictions for the end of the century saw the need to increase track capacity over much of the route.

Another alternative became apparent. A high speed line between Paris and Lyon could be built to avoid the need for costly expansions of the existing, indirect route. The line would be for passenger trains only, and would have its own special trains.

In 1972, SNCF introduced the prototype TGV, a gas turbine unit developed from the RTGs. Much equipment used on the final TGVs was tested in the prototype, all-electric TGVs. The prototype, TGV 001, is still used for continuing tests on the LGV but is now unpowered (and thus is not included in the book) and is towed by a conventional TGV for test runs.

Although the final production TGV units are moderately conventional, the line that they run on is quite different from 'conventional' railway lines. Rather than avoiding steep gradients by following circuitous routes or by tunnelling, the line is remarkably straight and has a profile like a roller coaster which includes gradients up to 1 in 28.5. This produced great savings in construction costs. And because of the straight route, lops 56 miles off the Paris-Lyon run, journey times can be much shorter. To make up for the gradients, TGV trains have a very high power/weight ratio. However, this has not meant that energy consumption on the new line is very high, as trains spend almost as much time coasting downhill as using power up the banks! An important feature of TGV units is that they can be used as easily off the new line as on it. The map below shows the new line, together with the route of the 'classic' Paris-Lyon line, and the branches now served by TGV.

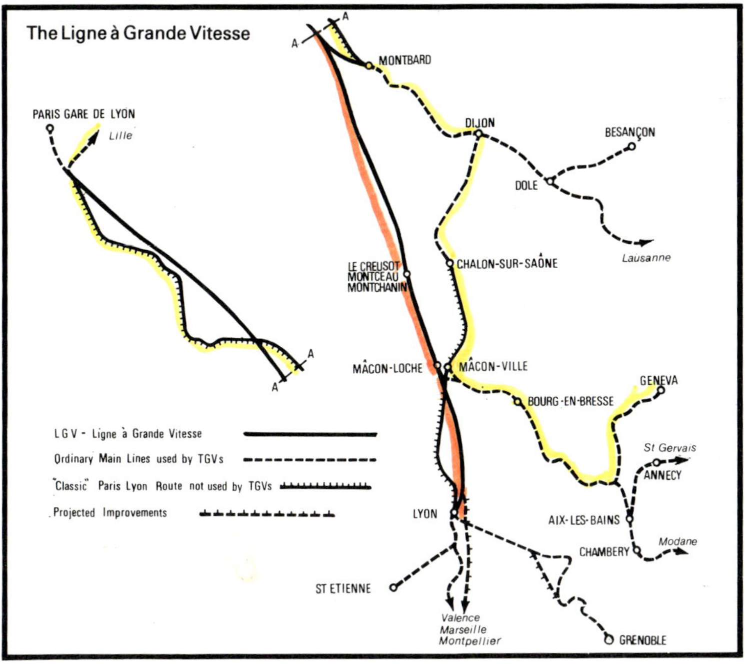

Bi-current & Tri-current First/Second Class Units

Car type:	TGV	*TGV*ZRADru
Number series:		
(01-32)	TGV 23001-063 (odd)	TGVZR 123001-032
(39-99)	TGV 23077-197 (odd)	TGVZR 123039-099
(110-117)	TGV 33001-015 (odd)	TGVZR 133001-008
Seating:	—	35 first

Bi-current First Class Units

Car type:	TGV	TGVZRADru
Number series:		
(33-38)	TGV 23065-075 (odd)	TGVZR 123033-038
(100-102)	TGV 23199-203 (odd)	TGVZR 123100-102
Seating:	—	35 first
Length:	22.15m (72ft 8in)	21.845m (71ft 8in)
Weight:	65 tonnes	43 tonnes

Permanent formation:
First/second class units –
TGV+ZRADru+RAru+RAu+RBrux+RBu+RBu+RBu+ZRBru+TGV
First class units –
TGV+ZRADru+RAru+RAu+RArux+RAu+RAu+RAru+ZRAru+TGV
Built by: Alsthom/MTE/De Dietrich
Introduced: 1978-86
UIC power rating (unit):
Under 1,500V dc – 3,100kW (4,160hp)
Under 25kV ac – 6,450kW (8,650hp)
Under 15kV ac – 2,800kW (3,760hp)

Maximum speed: 280km/h (174mph)
Pantograph types: Faiveley AMDE two-stage and AM18B single arms
Nominal supply voltages: 1,500V dc, 25kV 50Hz (& 15kV ac 16⅔Hz for 110-117)
Depot of allocation: PE
Works responsible: Paris Sud-Est TGV depot
Livery: Orange with dark grey window band and roof, narrow white band above and broad white band below windows

The TGV Fleet

The fleet of passenger TGVs consists of three different types which are, as far as possible, identical both mechanically and internally. TGV Nos 01-32 & 39-99 (96-99 are still under construction) are 'standard' units which operate off 1,500V dc or 25kV ac and which have both first and second class seating. TGV Nos 33-38 & 100-102 are identical mechanically but have all-first class seating. Finally, TGV Nos 110-117 (117 is still to be received) are tri-current units which can work off 15kV ac in order to operate to Lausanne in Switzerland, but are internally identical to the 'standards'. The main fleet has been in service since the full opening of the LGV in 1983, but since then SNCF has received a few more units in order to be able to augment capacity and expand services where required.

TGV Design

TGVs for the Paris Sud-Est scheme are 10-car units which consist of two power cars, each on two bogies, encasing eight trailer cars which are articulated, with bogies under the connections between coaches. One of the connections is seen opposite. The connecting wire carries the supply current from the pantograph to the second power car, thus avoiding the problems associated with two pantographs being used at the same time. Power cars contain most of the electrical equipment and are fitted with two pantographs each, one of which is a two-stage unit designed specially for high speed running on the LGV. The whole unit is heavily streamlined and trailer cars are lower and narrower than standard SNCF stock in order to reduce wind resistance. The extremities of power car noses open up to reveal Scharfenberg couplers (see photograph) which are used when a train runs in two sections or when capacity needs to be augmented.

*TGV*RAru	*TGV*RAu	*TGV*RBrux
TGVR 223001-032	TGVR 323001-032	TGVR 423001-032
TGVR 223059-099	TGVR 323039-099	TGVR 423039-099
TGVR 233001-008	TGVR 333001-008	TGVR 433001-008
38 first	38 first	35 second

*TGV*RAru	*TGV*RAu	*TGV*RArux
TGVR 223033-038	TGVR 323033-038	TGVR 423033-038
TGVR 223100-102	TGVR 323100-102	TGVR 423100-102
38 first	38 first	24 first
18.7m (61ft 4in)	18.7m (61ft 4in)	18.7m (61ft 4in)
28 tonnes	28 tonnes	29 tonnes

TGV Services

Services can be divided into four categories:

A The first only follow the LGV as far as Montbard then branch off to serve Dijon and destinations beyond. Of these, there are two trains a day which extend to Chalon-sur-Saône, three return journeys a day to Besançon and others which terminate at Dijon itself. The main service on this route, however, is that to Lausanne via Frasne. This is formed of TGV 33000 tri-current units and is worked by Swiss railwaymen between Vallorbe and Lausanne. Many of the trains on this route join or separate at Dijon.

B Trains which come off the LGV at Mâcon. These include four return journeys a day Paris-Geneva, all-the-year-round trains to Annecy and Chambéry plus 'TGV-Neige' services to St Gervais and Modane in the winter sports season.

C Services which pass through Lyon. A regular interval service exists between Paris and Lyon with certain trains extending to St Etienne, Valence or Grenoble. To these must be added Paris-Marseille (some of which extend to Toulon) and Paris-Montpellier trains, most of which pass through Lyon Part Dieu without stopping.

D Two trains a day (from June 1986) each way between Lyon and Lille. These trains take the LGV along its full length then the Grande Ceinture to avoid Paris and the Paris-Lille line at normal speeds.

Although services are now settling into a regular pattern, spare units will enable SNCF to extend existing services where thought appropriate. Changes may include additional Paris-Toulon and, perhaps, more 'TGV-Neige' services following present successes.

*TGV*RBu	*TGV*RBu	*TGV*RBu
TGVR 523001-032	TGVR 623001-032	TGVR 723001-032
TGVR 523039-099	TGVR 623039-099	TGVR 723039-099
TGVR 533001-008	TGVR 633001-008	TGVR 733001-008
60 second	60 second	60 second
*TGV*RAu	*TGV*RAu	*TGV*RAru
TGVR 523033-038	TGVR 623033-038	TGVR 723033-038
TGVR 523100-102	TGVR 623100-102	TGVR 723100-102
38 first	38 first	38 first
18.7m (61ft 4in)	18.7m (61ft 4in)	18.7m (61ft 4in)
28 tonnes	28 tonnes	28 tonnes

TGV-Atlantique and other Future TGV Lines

With the success of the TGV Sud-Est still fresh, SNCF are going ahead with a second high-speed line from Paris to the Rennes, Nantes and Bordeaux main lines. The new line will begin at Paris Montparnasse, follow a convenient disused trackbed through the suburbs then out into the open countryside following a common line before splitting into two branches which will join existing lines at Le Mans and Tours. Although not as long as the Paris-Lyon line, the scheme will allow dramatic journey time reductions. The line will differ from the Sud-Est LGV in having inclines limited to 1 in 55 and a few tunnels. In addition, the trains will be different in having 10 trailers instead of eight, as well as new micro-electronic control equipment and redesigned interiors. Trains will be capable of 300km/h (186mph). Services are expected to start in 1989 for the northern branch and 1990 for the southern leg. SNCF is also studying the possibility of other LGVs from Paris to Brussels with legs to Cologne and Amsterdam, and from Paris to Frankfurt via Metz.

TGV World Record

TGV 16 *Lyon* holds the world rail speed record of 380km/h (236mph) and, as the photograph shows, carries plates to advertise the fact. The record was set on the LGV on 26 February 1981 with the unit reduced in length, its bogies re-geared and the traction voltage boosted. Whatever the conditions, it shows that there is a large margin of safety built into the LGV. It should be noted that SNCF also holds the world record for an electric locomotive, which is jointly held by Nos BB 9004 and CC 7107.

*TGV*ZRBru
TGVR 823001-032
TGVR 823039-099
TGVR 833001-008
60 second

*TGV*ZRAru
TGVR 823033-038
TGVR 823100-102
38 first

21.845m (71ft 8in)
44 tonnes

TGV
TGV 23002-064 (even)
TGV 23078-198 (even)
TGV 33002-016 (even)
—

TGV
TGV 23066-076 (even)
TGV 23200-204 (even)
—

22.15m (72ft 8in)
65 tonnes

TGV Names
TGVs are not only named after the towns they regularly serve but have been baptised in towns elsewhere in order to promote the modern image of SNCF. Certain units have two names and one has three! Names are carried on the trailer cars behind the power cars and are stickers rather than the usual plates in order not to cause air resistance. This can be seen here, together with one of the units' sliding doors and retractable footsteps.

Here, TGVs Nos 50 and 87 wait to leave Paris Gare de Lyon, with the familiar station clock tower in the background.

Class TGV 923000 (TGV Postal)

Car types:	TGV	TGVZRP	TGVRP
Number series:	TGV 923001-5	TGVR 912301-5	TGVR 922301-5 TGVR 932301-5 TGVR 942301-5
Length:	[illegible]	21.845m (71ft 8in)	[illegible]
Weight:	65 tonnes	38 tonnes	19 tonnes

Formation: Ten-car (TGV+TGVZR+TGVR+TGVR+TGVR+TGVR+TGVR+TGVR+TGVZR+TGV)
Built by: Alsthom/MTE
Introduced: 1984
UIC power rating (unit):
Under 1,500V dc 3,100kW (4,160hp)
Under 25kV ac 6,450kW (8,650hp)

Maximum speed: 280km/h (174mph)
Pantograph type: Faiveley AMDE two-stage single-arm
Nominal supply voltages: 1,500V dc & 25kV ac 50Hz
Depot of allocation: PE
Works responsible: Paris Sud Est TGV depot
Livery: Canary yellow with dark grey roof, grilles on power car and around cab windows, lined in white and with 'La Poste' lettering and symbol in blue

The postal TGVs have been introduced in order for the French post office (PTT) to take advantage of the Ligne à Grande Vitesse to speed up and streamline their services on the Paris-Lyon corridor. For this they have bought two and a half TGV units, the half being in reserve for maintenance purposes. The units are basically the same as passenger TGVs except that they have no windows or seats and, instead, have facilities inside for holding specially designed containers for holding the mail. Unfortunately for the photographer, these units operate mainly in the late evening or at night. However, there is one working in the daytime, leaving Lyon at 10.18 and arriving in Paris at 12.44. The illustration (*SNCF/CAV/Bruno Vignal*) shows a rake at speed on the LGV.

Class 230 G

Number: 230 G 353
Built by: PO company
Introduced: 1923
Type: 4-6-0
Length (loco+tender): 17.733m (58ft 2in)
Wheelbase: 7.7m (25ft 3in)
Driving wheel diameter: 1.75m (5ft 9in)
Weight in running order (loco): 68 tonnes
Maximum speed: 100km/h (62mph)
Number of cylinders: 2
Cylinder diameter x Stroke: 500m x 650mm (19.7in x 25.6in)
Depot of allocation: Noisy-le-Sec (Paris)
Livery: Dark green with black smokebox, smoke deflectors and underframe lined in red and gold and with red buffer beam

No 230 G 353 is SNCF's only steam locomotive which is kept in regular service for specials, films etc, although there is a large collection on static display in the French National Railway Museum in Mulhouse. There also exists a large number of steam locomotives owned by societies or individuals which can often be seen on specials over SNCF metals. However, for SNCF-organised shows and open days it is usually No 230 G 353 which is wheeled out to do the honours.

In the photograph (*J.L. Chaigneau/SNCF*) 230 G 353 heads a special train of 1920s vintage double deck stock, the last of which was withdrawn from work out of St Lazare as late as 1984.

Names

All SNCF locomotive and unit names (except CC 6572 which is named after the railway resistance movement – *Résistance Fer*) are towns, départements or regions of France, or, in the case of tri-current TGVs, in Switzerland. The naming ceremonies are often connected with events or celebrations in the places concerned. Although the majority of locomotives or units are named after places where they regularly work, this is not always true and transfers from depot to depot further mix things up. However, TGV 50 is never likely to work under its own power to Beauvais and there are many more examples like this. It will also be noted that several towns have christened both a TGV and another loco. For example, TGV 02 and CC 72071 *Marseille*, TGV 42 and BB 7226 *Chambéry*, etc.

SNCF Depots

1 Eastern Region (Réseau Est)*
CH Chalindrey   MZ Metz
LV La Villette (Paris)   SG Strasbourg
MN Mohon   TV Thionville

2 Northern Region (Réseau Nord)*
LE La Chapelle (Paris)   LS Lens
LP La Plaine (Paris)   LU Longueau (Amiens)

3 Western Region (Réseau Ouest)
AS Achères (Paris)   NT Nantes Blottereau
CN Caen   RS Rennes
LM Le Mans   SE Sotteville (Rouen)
LR La Rochelle   SL St Lazare-Levallois (Paris)
MR Montrouge (Paris)

4 South Western Region (Réseau Sud Ouest)
BX Bordeaux   TB Tarbes
LA Les Aubrais (Orléans)   TE Toulouse
LI Limoges   TS Tours, St Pierre des Corps
PS Paris Sud Ouest   VV Villefranche le Conflent

5 South Estern Region (Réseau Sud Est)
AN Avignon   NI Nîmes
CY Chambéry   NS Nevers
DN Dijon Perrigny   PE Paris Sud Est (TGV)
LN Lyon Mouche   SB Saint Gervais les Bains
LY Lyon Vaise   VE Villeneuve St Georges (Paris)
ME Marseille Blancarde   VX Vénissieux (Lyon)

Note

The codes used are not official SNCF ones but were invented by the author for greater simplicity. The regional number codes are official and may be carried on locomotives, particularly on buffer beams.

*NB SNCF merged the Nord and Est regions at the start of 1985 but continues to refer to them separately.

SNCF Works

Béziers
Bordeaux
Epinay
Hellemmes (Lille)
Le Mans
La Folie (Paris)
Nevers
Oullins (Lyon)
Sotteville Quatre Mares (Rouen)
Vitry sur Seine (Paris)